All About the States Search-A-Word Puzzles

FRANK J. D'AGOSTINO

DOVER PUBLICATIONS, INC.
Mineola, New York

Bibliographical Note

All About the States Search-A-Word Puzzles is a new work, first published by Dover Publications, Inc., in 1996.

International Standard Book Number

ISBN-13: 978-0-486-29400-1
ISBN-10: 0-486-29400-5

Manufactured in the United States by Courier Corporation
29400510   2013
www.doverpublications.com

Publisher's Note

FRANK D'AGOSTINO has been creating search-a-word puzzles for nearly 25 years, since he was in the ninth grade, and he hasn't stopped yet. Over the years, he has put together more than 5,000 such puzzles on topics ranging from actors to zoo animals. Now he turns his attention to the states of the union, with a new collection of puzzles covering each state and the District of Columbia. These 51 puzzles will help you learn new words and test your knowledge of American history and geography. In working through these puzzles, you will learn about the principal cities of each state, their most important industrial and agricultural products, famous people who were born there, monuments and battlefields, as well as the state's official motto, song, bird, flower, even in some cases the state's official insect!

The format of the search-a-word puzzle is by now known to and enjoyed by millions of people. The words are given to the reader; you simply have to exercise your visual acuity and your ability to recognize patterns in order to solve the puzzle. Bear in mind that the words not only run vertically, horizontally and diagonally, but they may be spelled backwards as well. Words always run in a straight line and never skip letters. One letter may be used to form more than one word. Circle each word in the diagram and then cross it off the word list. If you get stuck, the correct answer patterns are included at the back of the book, beginning on page 55.

ALABAMA

Entered Union: Dec. 14, 1819 (#22)
Land Size: #28

ALABAMA (state song)
ALPINE (town)
ANNISTON (city)
AUBURN University
BIRMINGHAM (city)
CAMELLIA (state flower)
CATTLE (livestock)
Saltpeter CAVE
CHEAHA Mtn. (highest point)
COTTON (crop)
FLORENCE (city)
HELEN Keller's Birthplace
HUNTSVILLE (city)
MARBLE (state stone)

MILES College
MOBILE (city)
MONARCH Butterfly (state insect)
MONTGOMERY (capital)
MORRIS (town)
MOUND State Monument
ROYAL (town)
RUSSELL Cave Nat'l Monument
SELMA (city)
SEQUOYAH Cave
SOUTHERN PINE (state tree)
Jacksonville STATE University

TARPON (state saltwater fish)
TOMBIGBEE River
TROY State University
TUSKEGEE (town)
WARD (town)
WE DARE Defend Our Rights (state motto)
WING (town)
WINSTON 500 (auto race)
YARBO (town)
YELLOWHAMMER (state bird)

```
A U B U R N O T S N I W B T L
L L E S S U R A W I N G M O A
M A A T U S K E G E E O N M Y
I O Y B M H D M O U N D O B E
L A B O A A U B L T A N T I L
E L B I R M I N G H A M S G L
S C S E L M A O T R C O I B O
N H N A M E M I C S A R N E W
O E L E L E A H L E V R N E H
T A B T R N N O E L E I A L A
T H T Y E O B A T B E S L L M
O A O L P R L W A R D M P L M
C R E R A A L F T A A I A I E
T H A Y O U Q E S M N L B C R
B T A E N I P N R E H T U O S
```

ALASKA

Entered Union: Jan. 3, 1959 (#49)
Land Size: #1

ALASKA'S FLAG (state song)
ANCHORAGE (city)
BETHEL (town)
BOWHEAD WHALE (state marine mammal)
CRABS (product)
FORGET-ME-NOT (state flower)
GOLD (state mineral)
HAINES (town)
Alaska HIGHWAY
IDITAROD Trail Sled Dog Race

JADE (state gem)
JUNEAU (capital)
KENAI Mountains
KING SALMON (state fish)
Kukaklek LAKE
LAST FRONTIER State
MOUNT MCKINLEY (highest point)
Dog MUSHING (state sport)
NAKNEK Lake
NOME (city)
NORTH TO THE Future (state motto)

PALMER (town)
Brooks RANGE (mountains)
SITKA SPRUCE (state tree)
SLED races
VALDEZ (town)
WILLOW PTARMIGAN (state bird)
WOOLLY MAMMOTH (state fossil)
YUKON River

```
W O O L L Y M A M M O T H A L
I K S K A L E G A R O H C N A
L A Y E E G N A R J A L R L S
L E E A C N D K S U E D A J T
O L L F W U K O L N S S B K F
W A N O M H R A R E K L S R R
P H I R U A G P N A E L E K O
T W K G S S V I S U T M A D N
A D C E H A A F H A L I O S T
R A M T I H L A L A K A D N I
M E T M N A D S P S Y T K I E
I H N E G B E T H E L U I E R
G W U N O S Z A I A N E K S L
A O O O L K I N G S A L M O N
N B M T D E H T O T H T R O N
```

ARIZONA

Entered Union: Feb. 14, 1912 (#48)
Land Size: #6

ALAMO Reservoir
ARIZONA (state song)
AVONDALE (town)
BARTLETT Reservoir
Saguaro CACTUS Blossom
   (state flower)
CANELO (town)
CARDINALS (football)
San CARLOS Lake
CASA Grande (town)
CATTLE products
CHANDLER (town)
COLORADO River
COTTON (products)

GLENDALE (city)
GRAND CANYON State
HEARD Museum (Native
   American art)
LAKE Mohave
Lake MEAD
MESA (city)
NAVAJO National Monument
PALOVERDE (state tree)
PHOENIX (capital)
Lake POWELL
PRESCOTT (city)
RODEO shows
SALT River Valley

SCOTTSDALE (city)
Baseball SPRING TRAINING
Phoenix SUNS (basketball)
TEMPE (city)
TONTO National Monument
TUCSON (city)
TURQUOISE (state gem)
VERDE River
Cactus WREN (state bird)
YUMA (city)

```
S T U R Q U O I S E W R E N Z
U T A R O C A R D I N A L S E
T T E M P E P R C N A O A P L
C O T T O N E H A N J M D R A
A C I N Z V A M O A N A N I D
C S E I O N U Z V E M L O N S
I E D L D Y I A T E N A V G T
C R A L A R N Z S O A I A T T
O P E H A D S A S Z N A X R O
L R M E R O N C C E L T T A C
O N O A L O U E A D K Z O I S
R S A R R T D C L N N A A N N
A A A D Z I O E A G E A L I U
D C L L E W O P O S A L R N S
O N A Y T T E L T R A B O G R
```

ARKANSAS

Entered Union: June 15, 1836 (#25)
Land Size: #27

APPLE BLOSSOM (state flower)
ARKANSAS (state song)
BATESVILLE (town)
BENTON (town)
BOSTON Mountains
Lake CHICOT
COTTON (products)
DAISY (town)
DIAMOND (state gem)
DIAZ (town)
DUMAS (town)
DYESS (town)
EL DORADO (town)

Greers FERRY Lake
FORT SMITH (city)
HARDING University
HENDERSON State University
JACKSONVILLE (town)
KIRBY (town)
LITTLE ROCK (capital)
MAGAZINE Mountain (highest point)
MAGNET (town)
MARIE (town)
MOCKINGBIRD (state bird)
NIMROD Lake

Land of OPPORTUNITY State
OUACHITA River
OZARK Reservoir
PINE (state tree)
POULTRY (products)
REED (town)
RICE (crop)
Little RIVER
RODEO of the Ozarks
SOYBEANS (crop)
SPRINGDALE (town)

```
N D O R M I N O S R E D N E H
N O T N E B A T E S V I L L E
D U M A S K S E Y R T L U O P
O A H R A P D N R Z I A R D K
P D D T I K R G A V A E R Y R
P A S N I C C I N E V I O E A
O I E R O M E O N I B N D S Z
R S B T A M S S R G D Y E S O
T Y T R A K A T N E D R O A D
U O I G C S O I R O L A A S A
N E N A N C K S D O T T L H R
I E J A I C Y R R E F S T E O
T A K H O U A C H I T A O I D
Y R C M A G A Z I N E K S B L
A P P L E B L O S S O M R A E
```

CALIFORNIA

Entered Union: September 9, 1850 (#31)
Land Size: #3

ALBANY (town)
BELL (town)
BURBANK (city)
CALIFORNIA Valley Quail (state bird)
CERES (town)
CHICO (town)
CLOVIS (town)
CONCORD (town)
DESERT Tortoise (state reptile)
DIABLO Range
DISNEYLAND (theme park)
FRESNO (city)

GOLDEN STATE
HOLLYWOOD (studios)
I LOVE YOU, California (state song)
Los Angeles KINGS (hockey)
LODI (town)
LOS ANGELES (city)
MALIBU Beach
NATIVE Gold (state mineral)
St. Diego PADRES (baseball)
Golden POPPY (state flower)
California REDWOOD (state tree)
ROSE BOWL

SACRAMENTO (capital)
SERPENTINE (state rock)
STOCKTON Ship Canal
Movie STUDIOS
Golden TROUT (state fish)
TUNA (fish)
VENTURA (town)
YORBA LINDA (birthplace of Richard Nixon)
YOSEMITE Valley (highest US waterfall)
YUBA City (town)

```
L N R I A D N I L A B R O Y F
O R O D O O W Y L L O H O A R
D S S I V O L C U A V S C M E
I E E A W C O N K E E L A S
A R B C L D Y U I M N T A L N
B P O O E E T N I A T A B I O
L E W P V R G T I I U T U B T
O N L O O S E N R N R S Y U N
D T L U S P R S A F A N T R E
R I T F C O P T S S A E R B M
O N L H F A I Y M B O D E A A
C E I I D V I D L R O L S N R
N C L R E A C A U N L O E K C
O A E N O T K C O T S G D L A
C S A D N A L Y E N S I D A S
```

COLORADO

Entered Union: Aug. 1, 1876 (#38)
Land Size: #8

ADAMS State College
AQUAMARINE (state gem)
ASPEN (ski resort)
BENT'S Old Fort
BLUE Spruce (state tree)
BOULDER (city)
Lark BUNTING (state bird)
CATTLE (livestock)
CENTENNIAL State
CENTRAL CITY (town)
COLORADO River
Rocky Mtn. COLUMBINE
 (state flower)
CORN (crop)
DENVER (capital)

DINOSAUR National Park
 (fossils)
Mt. ELBERT (highest point)
GOLDEN (town)
The GREAT Plains
GREELEY (city)
Ft. LEWIS College
LORETTO Heights College
MESA Verde National Park
(US) MINT (Denver)
NOTHING Without
 Providence (state motto)
Denver NUGGETS
 (basketball)
(US) OLYMPIC Committee

Pikes PEAK
PUEBLO (state fair)
ROCKY MOUNTAINS
ROUTT county
ROYAL Gorge
SAWATCH Range (Rocky
 Mtns.)
SILT (town)
SKIER
STEGOSAURUS (state fossil)
STERLING (town)
VAIL (ski resort)
WARD (town)

```
B O U L D E R U A S O N I D C
A D A M S U R U A S O G E T S
C D O Y S V B U N T I N G A N
A A H C T A W A S C V N Q O I
R L T R E I K S A E T U O L A
L O E T R L C S R S A G T O T
A O S W L C P L E M E G T D N
I L T A I E O N A D R E E A U
N Y N R N S I R O R G T R R O
N M E D G B I L N T T S O O M
E P B L M N B A N U H N L L Y
T I B U E E S I O O T I E O K
N C L R U E M R O Y A L N C C
E O U P M T R E B L E L I G O
C P E A K E R G O L D E N S R
```

Entered Union: Jan. 9, 1788 (#5)
Land Size: #48

AIRCRAFT parts (products)
AMERICAN Robin (state bird)
BALD Mountain
BRISTOL (city)
CLAMS (product)
COAST GUARD Academy
CONNECTICUT River
CONSTITUTION State
DANBURY (city)
DENISON House (Mystic)
GARNET (state mineral)
HARTFORD (capital)
INDIAN Mountain

INSURANCE (industry)
LONG Island Sound
MARK Twain Mansion (Hartford home)
MILK (product)
MOUNTAIN LAUREL (state flower)
NATHAN Hale Homestead
NEW HAVEN (city)
NORWALK (city)
NUTMEG State
PACHAUG River
PINE Mountain
POULTRY (product)

PRAYING Mantis (state insect)
He Who Transplanted Still SUSTAINS (state motto)
THAMES River
TWIN Lakes
WATERBURY (city)
WHEAT (crop)
WHITE Oak (state tree)
YALE University
YANKEE Doodle (state song)

```
G A I R C R A F T I M I G G M
N A R F O S U S T A I N S U O
E N R I N D I A N I I S C A U
V D A N G S N Y Y N U O H N
A A A M E R I C A N O R C C T
H N E M C T N R L S R A O A A
W B T N T L P L E E W N A P I
E U W O I C O M E H A C S O N
N R I G C P A T A E L E T U L
T Y N T U H M R S T K K G L A
C O N S T I T U T I O N U T U
L D I K L F T U A H R K A R R
A L C K O T A E H W D B R Y E
M A Y R U B R E T A W N D A L
S B D E N I S O N A T H A N M
```

DELAWARE

Entered Union: Dec. 7, 1787 (#1)
Land Size: #49

AMERICAN Holly (state tree)
AMSTEL House (colonial arts)
ATLANTIC Ocean
BLUE HEN CHICKEN (state bird)
BROILER (chicken product)
CAMDEN (town)
CAPE Henlopen (state park)
CLAMS (product)
CORN (crop)
CRABS (product)
DELAWARE Seashore (state park)
DIAMOND State

DICKINSON House (built 1740)
DOVER (capital)
DUCK Creek
ELSMERE (town)
FIRST State
FORT Delaware (Civil War)
HAGLEY Museum (early mills)
HOGS (livestock)
LIBERTY And Independence (state motto)
LOWEST elevation in US
LUM'S POND

MILK (state beverage)
MUSHROOMS (crop)
NEW CASTLE (highest point)
OUR Delaware (state song)
PEACH Blossom (state flower)
Nanticoke RIVER
First Christmas SEAL
SOYBEANS (crop)
STATE HOUSE (Dover, built 1792)
Bay VIEW Beach
WEAKFISH (state fish)
WILMINGTON (city)

```
D E S U O H E T A T S E W O L
S E L T S A C W E N R O C N U
W I L M I N G T O N A L D O M
E E D A R E R E M S L E E S S
W S I N W C A B O G D H N N P
F E M V O A F U I O S A G I O
O E A O D M R A V H E M C K N
R A W K O E A E M B A Y I C D
T S R I F R R I Y S L T T I R
R Y R P E I H O D K T R N D E
S E E V E C S S I L A E A U L
B M I L A A L H U I D B L C I
A R A P G N C E J M W I T K O
R D E L O A P H A K L L A N R
C N E K C I H C N E H E U L B
```

American BEAUTY Rose (district flower)
BLAIR House (Vice President)
CAPITOL Building
Supreme COURT
DISTRICT of Columbia
FEDERAL Bureau of Investigation
FORD'S Theatre (Lincoln assassination)
(US) Botanic GARDEN
GEORGE Washington chose site
GOVERNMENT

HOUSE of Representatives
HOWARD University
JEFFERSON Memorial
JOHN (F.) Kennedy Center for the Performing Arts
JUSTICE FOR ALL (district motto)
LINCOLN Memorial
National MALL
MARYLAND (border)
METRO (subway)
NATIONAL Archives (houses documents)
OLD POST Office Building
POTOMAC River

SCARLET Oak (district tree)
(US) SENATE
SMITHSONIAN Institution
Air & SPACE Museum
STATE Dept.
TENLEYTOWN (highest point)
THOMAS Jefferson Memorial
Wood THRUSH (district bird)
UNION STATION (trains)
VOTE for President
WASHINGTON, D.C., (US capital)
WHITE House

```
L G A R D E N O S R E F F E J
I V B N O I T A T S N O I N U
N O S I N W O T Y E L N E T S
C T C A P I T O L O R T E M T
O E T D M C B L A I R O I G I
L T T R N O E T A T S T O O C
N A E J U O H F U R H V T F E
A N L B O O T T O S E T C G F
T E R E S H C G O R S D R I O
I S A A R I N N N O D O E D R
O U C U R E I M P I E S R F A
N O S T T A E D R G H A I U L
A H S Y N N L L A M W S M A L
L I P O T O M A C O S P A C E
D N A L Y R A M H E T I H W B
```

FLORIDA

Entered Union: March 3, 1845 (#27)
Land Size: #26

ALLIGATORS
Florida BALLET
BARRY College
Palm BEACH
Orange BLOSSOM (state flower)
BUSCH Gardens
CAPE Coral (town)
DADE County
EPCOT Center
FLORIDA KEYS (islands)
FT. MYERS (town)
GAINESVILLE (town)
Lake GEORGE
GULF of Mexico

HIALEAH (city)
HOGS (livestock)
Old Folks At HOME (Swanee River) (state song)
IN GOD WE TRUST (state motto)
St. JOHNS River
LARGEMOUTH BASS (freshwater fish)
LUMBER (products)
St. MARY'S River
MIAMI (city)
MOCKINGBIRD (state bird)
OCALA (town)
ORANGE (crop)

ORLANDO (city)
Sabal Palmetto PALM (state tree)
Florida PANTHER (state animal)
PEACE RIVER
PINE (tree)
PORT Charlotte (town)
SUGARCANE (crop)
SUNSHINE State
TALLAHASSEE (capital)
TAMPA (city)
WALTON (highest point)

```
P  L  S  R  E  Y  M  T  F  L  T  A  M  P  A
O  E  E  S  S  A  H  A  L  L  A  T  S  E  L
R  S  S  A  B  H  T  U  O  M  E  G  R  A  L
T  U  G  U  L  F  M  R  R  N  O  S  L  C  I
S  N  E  F  O  B  A  T  I  H  U  B  S  E  G
U  S  O  O  E  N  E  P  D  G  S  E  N  R  A
R  H  R  R  G  L  H  I  A  L  E  A  H  I  T
T  I  G  E  L  M  B  R  K  N  S  C  O  V  O
E  N  E  A  L  A  C  O  E  I  T  H  J  E  R
W  E  B  A  R  A  N  I  Y  P  M  H  P  R  S
D  F  P  R  N  D  A  D  S  R  C  A  E  O  Y
O  L  Y  E  W  A  L  T  O  N  C  O  I  R  R
G  A  I  N  E  S  V  I  L  L  E  A  T  M  A
N  E  D  A  D  R  I  B  G  N  I  K  C  O  M
I  E  M  O  H  C  S  U  B  L  O  S  S  O  M
```

ALBANY State College
ATHENS (city)
ATLANTA (capital)
AUGUSTA (city)
AZALEA (state wildflower)
BLUE Ridge Mountains
BROWN Thrasher (state bird)
CATFISH (product)
CATTLE (livestock)
CHEROKEE Rose (state flower)
COLUMBUS (city)
COTTON (crop)
DAHLONEGA (1st gold rush)
GAINESVILLE (town)
GEORGIA DOME (Falcons - football)
HIGH Museum of Art
HONEYBEE (state insect)
JEKYLL Island
JIMMY Carter (born in Plains)
Name: KING George (II) of Britain
LIVE OAK (state tree)
LOOKOUT Mountain
MACON (city)
MARTIN Luther King Center
MINING (industry)
OLYMPICS Games (1996)
Georgia ON MY MIND (state song)
PAINE College
PEACH State
PINE Forests
QUARTZ (gem)
RIGHT WHALE (marine mammal)
ROME (town)
SAVANNAH (city)
SHRIMP (crop)
VALDOSTA (town)
WISDOM, Justice, and Moderation (state motto)

```
J I M M Y H I G H S I F T A C
D E L L I V S E N I A G T A A
R N K V A L D O S T A N T S S
Z O I Y P M I R H S A T U C N
H T G M L O L G G L L B G I E
A E R N Y L E I T E M O R P H
N E I A I M I A V U G A T M T
N K G E U N N D L E Z U N Y A
A O H N N Q I O R A O W N L T
V R T R O I C M L K O A O O S
A E W T P C P E O R B E K K U
S H H E O A A O B L U E G I G
G C A I I C L M A R T I N N U
A C L N A G D A H L O N E G A
H E E B Y E N O H M O D S I W
```

HAWAII

Entered Union: Aug. 21, 1959 (#50)
Land Size: #47

AIEA (town)
ALOHA STATE
(U.S.S.) ARIZONA Memorial (Pearl Harbor)
AVOCADO (product)
BANANA (crop)
BISHOP Museum of Polynesian Ethnology & Natural History
CATTLE (livestock)
CHAMINADE University
COFFEE (product)
DIAMOND Head (extinct volcano)
DOLPHIN (fish)
FISH (industry)

Hawaiian GOOSE (state bird)
Pearl HARBOR (Oahu)
HAWAII'S OWN (state song)
HIBISCUS (state flower)
HILO (city)
HONOLULU (capital)
KAUAI (island)
KUKUI (Candlenut- state tree)
LAST STATE to enter
LIFE OF THE Land Is Perpetuated In Righteousness (state motto)
MARLIN (fish)
MAUI (island)
MILK (product)

MOLOKAI (island)
MOUNT Waialeale
NENE (Hawaiian goose)
NIIHAU (island)
PAPAYA (crop)
Sea Life PARK (aquarium)
PINEAPPLE (crop)
QUEEN EMMA Summer Palace (Hawaiian monarchy)
SUGAR CANE (crop)
TUNA (fish)
WAHIAWA (town)
WAILUKU (town)
WAIPAHU (town)

```
A A N I L R A M M E N E E U Q
W L H W B I S H O P L H U N I
D A O A A Y A P A P I A W E E
N R N H N A W R P C H O W N H
O I O I A A K A A I S A A E T
M Z L A N S E T I I I L M G F
A O U W A N T N I P A R O W O
I N L A I L W A A S H O U A E
D A U P E A W H T C S B N I F
O V K T A A U S H E R R T L I
L O K O H A T A E I U A M U L
P C L H L A I F K I W H G K I
H A I I T O F I S H I U K U K
I D M E H O M H I B I S C U S
N O A I C H A M I N A D E I A
```

IDAHO

Entered Union: July 3, 1890 (#43)
Land Size: #11

BARLEY (crop)
BEAR River
BIG WOOD River
BLACKFOOT River
Mountain BLUEBIRD (state bird)
BOISE (capital)
BORAH Peak (highest point)
CLEARWATER River
COEUR d'Alene (lake)
COLLEGE of Southern Idaho
COLUMBIA River
CRATERS Of The Moon National Monument

Seven DEVILS Mountains
Crystal FALLS Cave
GEM STATE
Fort HALL
HERE WE HAVE Idaho (state song)
IDAHO FALLS (city)
IT IS FOREVER (state motto)
LAVA Hot Springs
LEWIS And Clark Expedition
LOST River Mountains
Monument PEAK
PEAS (crop)
PEND Oreille Lake

POCATELLO (city)
PRIEST River
ROCKY Mountains
SALMON River
SHEEP Ranch
SUGAR Beets (crop)
SYRINGA (state flower)
TWIN Falls (city)
WHEAT (crop)
WHITE Pine (state tree)
WORLD CENTER for Birds of Prey
YELLOWSTONE Nat'l Park

```
W H E A T O L L E T A C O P W
O B A K S E V A H E W E R E H
R C O L A R S H E E P I B N I
L O D I L E A A N P E A S D T
D L R H S V P V O S I O I R E
C U S U A E T A T S M E G E S
E M L C E R R L S L L A F T L
N B I G W O O D W O I B D A L
T I V E C F C B O N A R G W A
E A E G R S K D L R I N A R F
R L D E A I Y I L B I W N A O
A T O L T T W E E R H O T E H
E S M L E I Y U Y S I W E L A
B O D O R T L S U G A R H C D
N L A C S B L A C K F O O T I
```

16

Chicago BEARS (football)
Chicago BULLS (basketball)
CARDINAL (state bird)
CHARLES MOUND (highest point)
CHICAGO (city)
COMISKEY Park (baseball White Sox)
DECATUR (city)
DICKSON Mounds Museum
DU SABLE Museum of African-American History
FIELD Museum of Natural History
GALENA (town)

Black HAWK Statue (Native American)
ILLINOIS (state song)
LAKE MICHIGAN
LINCOLN SHRINES
MOLINE (town)
NATIVE Violet (state flower)
O'HARE Airport
OHIO River
PEORIA (city)
PRAIRIE State
Ronald REAGAN (born in Tampico)
ROCK Island (town)
SHAWNEE Hills region

SOLDIER FIELD (Chicago football)
SOUTHLAWN (town)
SPRINGFIELD (capital)
STARVED Rock State Park
STATE Sovereignty, National Union (state motto)
STEPHEN Douglas Monument
URBANA (town)
VANDALIA Statehouse State Historic Site
WHITE OAK (state tree)
WRIGLEY Field (Chicago baseball)

```
P  D  U  S  A  B  L  E  N  O  S  K  C  I  D
S  E  N  I  R  H  S  N  L  O  C  N  I  L  N
O  V  O  N  W  A  L  H  T  U  O  S  O  E  U
A  R  W  R  D  L  E  I  F  S  O  H  I  P  O
N  A  R  H  I  L  Y  I  T  L  I  A  E  E  M
A  T  I  A  I  A  E  E  D  O  M  W  V  I  S
B  S  G  W  C  T  P  I  K  S  O  N  I  R  E
R  R  L  K  N  H  E  S  F  S  L  E  T  I  L
U  A  E  O  E  R  I  O  L  G  I  E  A  A  R
T  E  Y  N  F  O  O  C  A  S  N  M  N  R  A
A  B  O  I  N  I  I  H  A  K  E  I  O  P  H
C  U  E  I  A  N  E  L  A  G  D  N  R  C  C
E  L  L  S  N  A  G  A  E  R  O  C  K  P  I
D  L  A  I  L  A  D  N  A  V  E  T  A  T  S
I  S  N  A  G  I  H  C  I  M  E  K  A  L  S
```

ANGEL Mounds (archaeological finds)
BALL State University
On The BANKS Of The Wabash, Far Away (state song)
BROWN County State Park
CARDINAL (state bird)
CARR Lake
COAL (product)
CORN (crop)
CROSSROADS Of America (state motto)
Indiana DUNES National Lakeshore Preserve
ELECTRICAL equipment (product)
FRANKLIN Township (highest point)
FT. WAYNE (city)
GARY (city)
GOSHEN College
Benjamin HARRISON home
HOGS (livestock)
HOOSIER State
INDIANAPOLIS (capital)
Indiana means LAND of Indians
Abraham LINCOLN'S Boyhood Home
METALS (product)
OHIO River
PEONY (state flower)
PERU (town)
RECTANGLE (shape)
RUSH County
SAND Dunes (Lake Michigan)
SANTA Claus (town)
SOUTH Bend (city)
SOYBEANS (crop)
Indianapolis SPEEDWAY
TERRE Haute (city)
TULIP (state tree)
WABASH River
WASHINGTON (town)
WEST Baden Springs (town)
WHEAT (crop)
WHITEWATER River

```
O E S T N O T G N I H S A W H
I L I L U H T U O S O I S E S
H E N R A L L D N H O N K S U
O C L R L T I A U S S N T R
F T W A Y N E P A N I A A N E
R R B C N B L M I L E N B L T
A I A I Y D G Y O O R S A A A
N C N O B S N P A C I I Y N W
K A S R C O A L N N S A R I E
L L O O E N T N D I G T A D T
I W R P A I C A T L O E G R I
N N E I W H E A T A H R L A H
A R D H A R R I S O N R N C W
U N E H S O G Y A W D E E P S
I N D N A S D A O R S S O R C
```

ADVENTURELAND (Altoona)
BLUE Lake
BRIAR CLIFF College
CEDAR RAPIDS (city)
Sioux CITY (city)
CORALVILLE Reservoir
CORN (crop)
COUNCIL Bluffs (city)
DAVENPORT (city)
DES MOINES (capital)
EASTERN Goldfinch (state bird)
FARM machinery (products)

HAWKEYE State
HOGS (livestock)
Herbert HOOVER (born in West Branch)
INSURANCE (industry)
IOWA CITY (town)
Our LIBERTIES We Prize And Our Rights We Will Maintain (state motto)
LUTHER College
Mt. MERCY College
MILK (product)
OAK TREE
OSCEOLA (highest point)

River OTTER (mammal)
SIMPSON College
SKUNK River
SONG Of Iowa (state song)
SOYBEANS (crop)
STORM Lake
TURKEY River
UNIVERSITY of Iowa
WATERLOO (city)
WESTMAR College
WHITE-TAILED Deer (livestock)
WILD Rose (state flower)

```
N  R  E  T  S  A  E  C  N  A  R  U  S  N  I
H  O  G  S  O  Y  B  E  A  N  S  T  A  O  B
W  A  T  E  R  L  O  O  W  T  R  L  W  S  R
H  D  L  N  I  B  A  K  U  O  U  A  I  D  I
I  V  I  I  O  L  N  R  P  T  C  S  L  I  A
T  E  C  O  B  U  K  N  H  I  W  O  D  P  R
E  N  N  M  K  E  E  E  T  R  S  N  O  A  C
T  T  U  S  Y  V  R  Y  E  C  K  G  M  R  L
A  U  O  E  A  W  C  T  E  L  I  T  R  R  I
I  R  C  D  H  R  T  O  I  K  S  A  O  A  F
L  E  W  M  E  O  L  M  R  E  W  O  T  D  F
E  L  R  M  O  A  O  I  W  N  S  A  S  E  I
D  A  C  O  R  A  L  V  I  L  L  E  H  C  W
F  N  O  S  P  M  I  S  E  E  R  T  K  A  O
A  D  C  I  T  Y  T  I  S  R  E  V  I  N  U
```

KANSAS

Entered Union: Jan. 29, 1861 (#34)
Land Size: #13

AIRCRAFT (producer)
ATCHISON (town)
BAKER University
BEAVER Creek
BETHEL College
CATTLE (livestock)
CORN (crop)
COTTONWOOD (state tree)
DODGE City
EISENHOWER Library (Abilene)
EL DORADO (town)
FLINT Hills (town)
FRIENDS University

FRONT STREET (Dodge City)
GARDEN City (town)
GRAIN (crop)
GREAT PLAINS
HOGS (livestock)
KANSAS CITY (city)
KINGMAN (town)
KIOWA (town)
LADDER Creek
LAKE McKinney
Western MEADOWLARK (state bird)
MOUNT Sunflower (highest point)

Wild NATIVE Sunflower (state flower)
PITTSBURG (town)
Home On The RANGE (state song)
SALINE River
ST. MARY College
Wichita STATE University
STERLING College
SUNFLOWER State
TOPEKA (capital)
WHEAT (crop)
WICHITA (city)

```
R E W O H N E S I E N I L A S
L N E D R A G N I L R E T S A
E A W S A K R A L W O D A E M
H V K H R N U S D O D G E S S
T O I E E S B A G C K L A N U
E D K T P A S Y O O T L I O N
B A N A A O T T L T H A R S F
B R R N S N T I A A L D C I L
E O C A U O I C H P N D R H O
A D A O N Y P S T C F E A C W
V L M W R G K A T L I R F T E
E E O A R N E S I A S W T A R
R O M A F R O N T S T R E E T
D T I A G N T A F R I E N D S
S N K A W O I K I N G M A N A
```

20

ABRAHAM LINCOLN (born in Hodgenville)
BIG SOUTH Fork National River & Recreation Area
BLUEGRASS State
Daniel BOONE National Forest
BOWLING Green (city)
CARDINAL (state bird)
CATTLE (livestock)
CHURCHILL Downs (horse race track)
COAL (product)
Kentucky COFFEE Tree (state tree)

CORN (crop)
COVINGTON (city)
EASTERN Mountain
FLORAL Clock (Frankfort attraction)
FRANKFORT (capital)
FT. KNOX (gold)
GOLDENROD (state flower)
HOGS (livestock)
My Old Kentucky HOME (state song)
HOPKINSVILLE (city)
KENTUCKY DERBY
LAKE Cumberland
LEXINGTON (city)

LOUISVILLE (city)
Black MOUNTAIN (highest point)
OHIO River
OWENSBORO (city)
RUPP Arena
SHAKER VILLAGE (Harrodsburg area settlement)
SOYBEANS (crop)
UNITED We Stand, Divided We Fall (state motto)

```
A N E G A L L I V R E K A H S
N B I G S O U T H T X T Y S M
G T R S N A E B Y O S B A E E
O N T A D E T I N U R R A L L
L L I R H N U K E E G S L E L
D A L L O A T K D E T I N X I
E N O I W F M Y U E V O L I V
N I R C H O K L R S O E A N S
R D O A K C B N I B C M R G N
O R B T U O R U A N E O O T I
D A S T K A O U Y R C H L O K
L C N L I L U I H U F O F N P
A E E E P P U R H C T G L N O
K T W N I A T N U O M S K N H
E N O T G N I V O C O F F E E
```

LOUISIANA

Entered Union: Apr. 30, 1812 (#18)
Land Size: #33

ACADIAN House Museum
  (Henry Wadsworth
  Longfellow)
AMITE River
ATCHAFALAYA River
BALD CYPRESS (state tree)
BATON ROUGE (capital)
BATTLE of New Orleans
BAYOU State
BEAVER (animal)
Eastern BROWN Pelican
  (state bird)
CATFISH (product)
Lake CHARLES
COAL (product)
CORN (crop)

COTTON (crop)
CRAB (product)
DRISKILL Mountain (highest
  point)
GIVE ME Louisiana (state
  song)
HOGS (livestock)
HOUMA (town)
LAKE Arthur
LOUISIANA State Museum
LUMBER (product)
MAGNOLIA (state flower)
METAIRIE (city)
Gulf of MEXICO
MONROE (city)
NEW ORLEANS (city)

PAPER (products)
PELICAN State
RICE (crop)
Red RIVER Valley
New Orleans SAINTS
  (football)
SHREVEPORT (city)
SOYBEANS (crop)
SUGAR CANE (crop)
SUPERDOME, New Orleans
  (1997 Super Bowl)
UNION, Justice, Confidence
  (state motto)

```
S N A E L R O W E N W O R B L
S S I I L L C H A R L E S O H
A U O S L R I C O B O M U S L
I T H Y E O I K A G E I I E S
N H C B B L N T S T S F C S H
T O M H E E O G A I T I E U R
S U T P A N A I A A R R M G E
L M S T R F R N C M P D E A V
A A B O O I A O S Y U E X R E
K I U E E C I L C G L O I C P
E G C O A L R D A T I V C A O
E T A D Y V L A T Y E V O N R
N O I N U A E A B R A L E E T
N A N M B A B R E O R N O M S
N R E P A P S U P E R D O M E
```

22

ACADIA National Park
ANDROSCOGGIN River
APPALACHIAN Mtns.
APPLE (crop)
AUGUSTA (capital)
BANGOR (city)
BAR HARBOR (town)
BATES College
BLACK Mansion (resembles Mt. Vernon)
BOOTHBAY Harbor (town)
BORDERS 1 state (NH)
CAMDEN (town)

CANADA border
CHICKADEE (state bird)
Mt. DESERT Island
State HOUSE
I DIRECT (state motto)
St. JOHN River
Mt. KATAHDIN (highest point)
KENNEBUNKPORT (town)
LEWISTON (city)
LUMBER (products)
State Of MAINE Song
State MUSEUM

NASSON College
PAPER (products)
PINE TREE State
POND Island
PORTLAND (city)
SEBAGO Lake
SKOWHEGAN (town)
Earliest SUNRISE
WHITE Pine Cone and Tassel (state flower)

```
A C A D I A S B R A D A N A C
U N A I H C A L A P P A P O H
G I D I R E C T O N B T A G I
U B O R D E R S N M G R N A C
S L D N O P Y A B H T O O B K
T E R M C S S K E S B P R E A
A W O D M S C P K B A K E S D
E I B S O A I O M K T N S T E
T S R N L N W R G U E U I J E
W T A B E H E T E G S B R R S
H O H T E P R L Y W I E N E U
I N R G A E P A J O H N U B O
T E A P S P E N I A M N S M H
E N B E A N E D M A C E M U I
U F D G N I D H A T A K H L V
```

23

MARYLAND

Entered Union: Apr. 28, 1788 (#7)
Land Size: #42

ANDREWS Air Force Base
ANNAPOLIS (capital)
APPALACHIAN Mountains
BACKBONE Mountain
(highest point)
BALTIMORE (city)
"BIRDS" (baseball Orioles)
BLACK-EYED SUSAN (state
flower)
CAMP DAVID (President's
retreat)
CHESAPEAKE Bay
CHOPTANK River
CRABS (product)
Manly DEEDS, Womanly
Words (state motto)

ENOCH Pratt Free Library
(Baltimore)
FREE State
GODDARD Space Flight
Center
HOOD College
JOHNS Hopkins University
Old LINE State
LOYOLA College
MARYLAND, My Maryland
(state song)
MASON-Dixon Line
MIDDLE River (town)
MILK (product)
NANTICOKE River
(US) NAVAL Academy

Baltimore ORIOLE (state bird)
OYSTERS
Agricultural RESEARCH
Service
Potomac RIVER
SILVER Spring (city)
STAR SPANGLED Banner (by
Francis Scott Key near
Baltimore)
SUSQUEHANNA River
TOWSON (city)
WHITE Oak (state tree)

```
M A S O N A I H C A L A P P A
B I C H E S A P E A K E S N D
L B L L I N E M H L N B N O M
A A H K A L A C D O C A H S N
C L A C D N R V H Y P W O W A
K T D D O A N E A O A H J O N
E I I E E N L A L L P I S T T
Y M S S E O E I H R E T B M I
E O E W I D S N O E L E A D C
D R S R E T S Y O Y U R R N O
S E O B I R D S D B Y Q C F K
U V D R A D D O G L K R S E E
S I L V E R J N A G Y C F U I
A R L D E L G N A P S R A T S
N A C A M P D A V I D H M B A
```

John ADAMS (born in Braintree)
ALL HAIL to Massachusetts (state song)
AMERICAN ELM (state tree)
BAY STATE
BLACK Heritage Trail
BOSTON (capital)
BY THE SWORD We Seek Peace, But Peace Only Under Liberty (state motto)
CAPE COD section
CHICKADEE (state bird)
CLARK University
Old COLONY State

COMMONWEALTH
DAIRY (product)
GARDNER Museum
Faneuil HALL (historic)
Bunker HILL (monument)
LADYBUG (state insect)
LENOX (city)
LOWELL (city)
MARTHA'S VINEYARD (island)
MASSACHUSETTS Bay
MAYFLOWER (state flower)
MERRIMACK River

MOUNT Greylock (highest point)
NANTUCKET (island)
Boston POPS
SALEM (city)
SCALLOPS (product)
SMITH College
SPRINGFIELD (city)
TUFTS University
WARE River
Right WHALE (state marine mammal)

```
M S N O T E E D A K C I H C A
A E T A T S Y A B H D A H L S
R U G U B Y D A L R L T L T B
T R L O W E L L O L L H F M L
H T E M E R A W A A A U D N A
A N N L M S E E I T L A S C
S O O H D E A W L W E N P Y K
V T X C H R N Y H I T O U N C
I S E T S O A A F U L S S O A
N O Y M M K L G C L H P S L M
E B A M R E N K A I O I A O I
Y D O A T I E C S P R W L C R
A C L A R T S M I T H E E L R
R C A P E C O D A I R Y M R E
D S S T T E S U H C A S S A M
```

MICHIGAN

Entered Union: Jan. 26, 1837 (#26)
Land Size: #22

ANN ARBOR (city)
APPLE Blossom (state flower)
Mt. ARVON (highest point)
AUTO (industry)
BATTLE Creek (city)
CONCORDIA College
CORN (crop)
DEARBORN (city)
DETROIT (city)
Tahquamenon FALLS
FERNDALE (town)
FLINT (city)
Gerald FORD Presidential
  Library

GRAND RAPIDS (city)
HENRY Ford Museum (cars)
HOUGHTON Lake
IF YOU SEEK a Pleasant
  Peninsula, Look About You
  (state motto)
KALAMAZOO (city)
LADY of the Lake State
LAKE Michigan
LANSING (capital)
MANISTEE National Forest
MICHIGAN MY Michigan
  (state song)
MILK (product)

MINING (industry)
MOUNT Clemens (city)
OTTAWA National Forest
ROBIN (state bird)
SAGINAW River
Detroit TIGERS (baseball)
TROUT (state fish)
WARREN (city)
WHITE Pine (state tree)
WOLVERINE State

```
N W H I T E K E E S U O Y F I
O O Z A M A L A K B M S O Y N
O L T Y A P P L E I K T M R A
T V A H A R V O N K T N O N B
U E M D G G I I N A A C U S A
A R A N Y U N F W G S L N D T
I I N T A G O A I C L I T I T
D N I I R R L H H D L W D P L
R E S G D O C A E I A O M A E
O R T E C I B A N N F I T R J
C R E R M R R R I S R E U D T
N A E S O B B G A M I Y H N U
O W A B O I A R T N I N I A O
C N I R M S T H G A N L G R R
T N N E L A D N R E F A K G T
```

26

BARLEY (crop)
BLOOMINGTON (city)
BREAD and Butter State
CHEESE (product)
COMPUTER (product)
CORN (crop)
CROW Wing River
DULUTH (city)
EAGLE Mountain (highest point)
High FALLS
(US) Hockey Hall of FAME
GARY (town)
GOPHER State
GRAND Portage National Monument
HAIL Minnesota (state song)

HAMLINE University
HONEY (product)
IRON Ore (leading US producer)
Pink and White LADY'S SLIPPER (state flower)
LAKE Superior
LAND Of 10,000 Lakes (nickname)
LOON (state bird)
LUMBER (products)
MILK (state beverage)
MINNEAPOLIS (city)
MINNEHAHA Falls
MINNESOTA Twins (baseball)
NORTH Star State

OATS (crop)
St. OLAF College
Red PINE (state tree)
POTATO (crop)
Red RIVER of the North
SIBLEY House (early State House)
ST. CLOUD (city)
ST. PAUL (capital)
STAR of the North (state motto)
SUGAR BEETS (crop)
TWIN Cities (Minneapolis & St. Paul)
VOYAGEURS National Park
WHEAT (crop)

```
Y L O O N O T G N I M O O L B
E E A T T N A G O O D H I R A
L S N D R R O A F N A F E E R
B U A O Y P T K A M M A A T L
I G C S H S L L L O D L G U E
S A G E I N S I O I N L L P Y
A R R R E L N L A O M S E M V
H B E A A E O T I H T S S O W
A E V B T N O P E P T A Y C O
H E I S M S D S A C P A T N R
E T R N E U E U L E G E S O C
N S O N L E L O E E N E R R P
N R N U H B U K U I M N M T I
I I T C T D A R W T N A I H N
M H A N A L S T A E H W F M E
```

MISSISSIPPI

Entered Union: Dec. 10, 1817 (#20)
Land Size: #31

BELHAVEN College
BIG BLACK River
CIVIL WAR Nat'l Battlefield
CLARKSDALE (city)
CORN (crop)
COTTON (crop)
DELTA National Park
EAGLE State
EGGS (product)
GRAND VILLAGE (Native American heritage)
GULF Islands (National Seashore)
Bluff HILLS region
JACKSON (capital)

LAUREL (city)
LEAF River
Evergreen MAGNOLIA (state flower)
MERIDIAN (city)
MILK (state beverage)
Go, MISSISSIPPI (state song)
MOCKINGBIRD (state bird)
NATCHEZ (city)
PACE (town)
PEARL RIVER
PREHISTORIC Whale (state fossil)
RANKIN (town)
RICE (crop)

ROWAN OAK (National Park area)
RUST College
SOYBEANS (crop)
Holly SPRINGS National Park
STATE Historical Museum
By VALOR and Arms (state motto)
WHEAT (crop)
WILD Duck (state waterfowl)
WOODHALL Mountain (highest point)

```
M O C K I N G B I R D S I L B
E I P F A E L C S S S I L N I
R T S U R E I P E O E A R I G
I B P S R V R G Y T H O U K B
D M E U I I G B A D C R E N L
I S A L N S E T O I E C L A A
A L W G H A S O S V I J A R C
N A S N N A W I I R S A D O K
R M R S O O V R P L P C S W L
W I L D M T L E L P S K K A I
H V A L O R T I N P I S R N M
E E L G A E H O A I M O A O F
A T L E D Z E H C T A N L A L
T S P R E H I S T O R I C K U
P A C E G A L L I V D N A R G
```

BLUEBIRD (state bird)
St. Louis BLUES (hockey)
BRANSON (town)
BULLION State
St. Louis CARDINALS (baseball)
CAVE State
CORN (crop)
COTTON (crop)
FLOWERING Dogwood (state tree)
HAWTHORN (state flower)
HOGS (livestock)
JEFFERSON City (capital)
KANSAS CITY (city)
LEAD State

MEAT Packing (industry)
MEXICO (town)
MISSOURI WALTZ (state song)
OSAGE River
OZARK State
PRAIRIE Home (town)
St. Louis RAMS (football)
Kansas City ROYALS (baseball)
SHOW ME State
SOYBEANS (crop)
SPRINGFIELD (city)
ST. JOSEPH (city)
ST. LOUIS (city)
Missouri STATE Museum

Let The Welfare Of The People Be The SUPREME Law (state motto)
TAUM SAUK Mountain (highest point)
Harry TRUMAN (born in Lamar)
TURKEY (livestock)
Name: Muddy WATER (Missouri River - Algonquin Indian)
WHEAT (crop)
WHITE RIVER region
Trans WORLD Dome (football Rams)

```
B E R I Y T I C S A S N A K F
L R M E X I C O Z I O R D L L
U N A E W H E A T I E L O E C
E O R N R A M S L T R W I A A
B S Z O S P R L A O E R Y D R
I R O A C O U W W R I E C O D
R E E Y R B N S I A K O Y E I
D F S V B K I N R R T A M S N
O F M S I E G P U T L W T E A
S E V A C R A T O S O L R U L
O J O S A G E N S H O I U L S
K U A S M U A T S U M T M B G
U D L E I F G N I R P S A I O
H P E S O J T S M H R M N E H
S T A T E N R O H T W A H O M
```

MONTANA

Entered Union: Nov. 8, 1889 (#41)
Land Size: #4

ASPEN (tree)
BARLEY (crop)
Grizzly BEAR (state animal)
BIG SKY Country (nickname)
BIGHORN Canyon
BILLINGS (city)
BITTERROOT (state flower)
BONANZA State
BUFFALO (town)
BUTTE (city)
CHERRY (crop)
COBB Field
COPPER (products)
FORT Benton
GOLD And Silver (state motto)

GREAT FALLS (city)
HELENA (capital)
Big HOLE Peak
LAND Of The Shining Mountains
LEWIS and Clark (National Historic Trail)
Montana MELODY (ballad)
MILK River
MISSOULA (city)
MONTANA (state song)
MOUNTAIN State
OATS (crop)
Crazy PEAK
Fort PECK Lake
Ponderosa PINE (state tree)

RED LODGE (town)
SAPPHIRE (gem)
SHEEP (livestock)
STUB TOE State
TETON River
TREASURE State
WESTERN Meadowlark (state bird)
WHEAT (crop)
WHITEFISH (product)
YELLOWSTONE National Park

```
A  E  O  T  B  U  T  S  G  N  I  L  L  I  B
L  G  C  W  N  U  O  K  C  E  P  N  H  T  I
U  D  H  O  E  R  F  N  D  E  O  Y  S  M  T
O  O  E  E  B  S  O  F  E  N  K  E  I  B  T
S  L  R  T  R  B  T  H  A  S  A  L  F  O  E
S  D  R  E  T  U  S  E  G  L  K  L  E  N  R
I  E  Y  L  N  U  S  I  R  I  O  O  T  A  R
M  R  S  O  A  B  B  A  S  N  B  W  I  N  O
E  R  I  H  P  P  A  S  E  T  M  S  H  Z  O
L  R  W  A  E  N  I  R  N  R  A  T  W  A  T
O  E  E  M  A  L  M  N  L  O  T  O  H  S  I
D  P  L  T  K  T  E  B  E  E  T  N  E  P  D
Y  P  N  N  M  T  E  N  O  A  Y  E  A  E  L
M  O  U  N  T  A  I  N  A  F  O  R  T  N  O
M  C  T  N  R  S  L  L  A  F  T  A  E  R  G
```

NEBRASKA

Entered Union: Mar. 1, 1867 (#37)
Land Size: #15

AGATE FOSSIL Beds (National Monument)
AGRICULTURE (industry)
AMERICAN Bison (animal)
ANTELOPE State
BEAUTIFUL Nebraska (state song)
BELLEVUE (town)
BLUE Agate (state gem)
CATTLE (livestock)
CORNHUSKER State
COTTONWOOD (state tree)
DAIRY (products)
DARR (town)

EQUALITY Before The Law (state motto)
GAGE County
GERALD FORD (born in Omaha)
GOLDENROD (state flower)
GRAIN (crop)
GRAND Island (town)
KEYA Raha River
LINCOLN (capital)
MISSOURI River
University of NEBRASKA
NORTH Platte (town)
OMAHA (city)

OVERLAND Trail
PERU State College
PHEASANT
PLATTE River
PONCA (town)
Name: Broad RIVER (Omaha Indian)
TREE PLANTERS State
Harold WARP Pioneer Village
WESTERN Meadowlark (state bird)
WHITE-TAILED Deer (state mammal)

```
T R L I S S O F E T A G A D N
R E K S U H N R O C B C R L E
E K R D N A L R E V O O O U L
E A A R K E Y A Y T F C V W T
P G K K B A P R T D N E H M T
L R O B S E I O L I L I A I A
A I M L R A N A L L T S E S C
N C A U D W R U E E A T E S E
T U H E O E F B T M T K Q O G
E L A O G I N A E A S N U U A
R T D W T O I R L N D N A R G
S U A U R L I P O N C A L I R
A R A T E C R R A D N E I V A
P E H D A P H E A S A N T E I
B R B N R E T S E W E R Y R N
```

31

NEVADA

Entered Union: Oct. 31, 1864 (#36)
Land Size: #7

ALL FOR OUR Country (state motto)
ANAHO Island Refuge
BARLEY (crop)
Great BASIN National Park
BATTLE BORN State
BLACK Rock Mountains
BUTTE Mountains
CARSON CITY (capital)
CATTLE (livestock)
Lehman CAVES National Monument
COPPER (mineral)
COTTON (product)
DESERT Bighorn Sheep (state animal)

ELKO (city)
GEYSER BASIN
GOLD (mineral)
HOME MEANS Nevada (state song)
HOOVER Dam
JACKSON Mountains
LAKE TAHOE
LAS VEGAS (city)
Lake MEAD Reservoir
MOUNTAIN Bluebird (state bird)
NEVADA Art Gallery
PARADISE (city)
Boundary PEAK (highest point)

RENO (city)
RODEO shows
Mt. ROSE
RUBY Mountain
SAGEBRUSH (state flower)
SHEEP
SILVER State
SINGLE-LEAF piñon (state tree)
SKIING
Name: "SNOWY" (Spanish)
SUN VALLEY (town)
VIRGINIA City (town)
WHITE River

```
A O H A N A I N I G R I V K N
N N I A T N U O M E V D H A Y
R E A H O O V E R Y E O H E B
O O V D E S O R E S M S L P U
B P D A V K A L E E U R R P R
E A N E D C L R M R A S E S A
L R E M O A T E B B D E P I L
T A T O V J A E D A H V P N L
T D T N H N G L N S D A O G F
A I U E S A O N S I I C C L O
B S B R S G T T I N S L V E R
L E L T T A C E T I O A V L O
A D W H I T E L K O K W B E U
C Y T I C N O S R A C S Y A R
K E D S A G E V S A L D E F V
```

BAKER River
BEAVER (animal)
BLACK BEAR (animal)
BLANKETS (product)
BOBCAT (animal)
CONCORD (capital)
CORN (crop)
CURRIER Gallery Of Art
White-tailed DEER (state animal)
EGGS (product)
Purple FINCH (state bird)
FORT Constitution
GRANITE State

HAMPTON (town)
HORSE (animal)
KEENE State College
LAKE Winnipesaukee
Purple LILAC (state flower)
LIVE FREE OR DIE (state motto)
MAPLE Syrup (product)
MERRIMACK River
MINING (industry)
NASHUA (city)
NEW HAMPSHIRE Hills (state song)
NORTH Hampton (town)

PAPER (industry)
PEACHES (crop)
RIVIER College
Arts and SCIENCE Center
SHEEP (livestock)
SKUNK (animal)
SULLIVAN (town)
THEATER BY the Sea
UMBAGOG Lake
Mt. WASHINGTON (highest point)
WHITE BIRCH (state tree)

```
B G O G A B M U N E F E T C N
O P H C R I B E T I H W H U O
B H E R N W H I N N D E E R T
C A L I L S N C K E R L A R G
A H N S D A H C S I O P T I N
T G S A R R A R H N C A E E I
R L G G S M O S E H N M R R H
E A G H I H P E A P O W B M S
P K E R T M U M E K C R Y P A
A E R R A R P A N R O C H A W
P E O H I T C U E S F O R T E
M N W V O H K V E C N E I C S
W E I N E S A S U L L I V A N
N E E S T E K N A L B R N I H
R E K A B L A C K B E A R S L
```

ATLANTIC City (city)
CAMDEN (city)
CHEMICAL (product)
CHERRY Hill (town)
Jersey CITY (city)
CLAM State
Grover CLEVELAND (born in Caldwell)
DELAWARE Water Gap
(NJ) DEVILS (hockey)
DREW University
EASTERN Goldfinch (state bird)
FORD Mansion (Morristown Nat'l Historical Park)

GARDEN State
GEORGE Washington Bridge
GIANTS Stadium (football)
HIGH POINT (highest point)
HORSE (state animal)
JOCKEY Hollow Trail
LAKE Hopatcong
LIBERTY And Prosperity (state motto)
MENLO PARK (Edison inventions)
MONTCLAIR Art Museum
NEW JERSEY State Museum
NEWARK (city)
New Jersey State OPERA

PAPER Mill Playhouse
PATHWAY of the Revolution State
PINE Barrens section
PURPLE Violet (state flower)
Northern RED OAK (state tree)
RUTGERS University
SETON HALL University
TRENTON (capital)
UNION (town)
WATERLOO Village
WICK House
WOODBRIDGE (town)

```
G A R D E N C N K Y E E K A L
I P K E W I O R E D O A K I N
A I R J T I A K E Y R C B D H
N N A Y N W C V Y I L E R I O
T E P U E O I E A A R E G E R
S G O N J L T L M T W H S D S
R D L O S E C N Y Y P H E E E
E I N R O T A C E O R O T L E
G R E A N L H S I R S P O A L
T B M O L E R N T T T E N W P
U D M D R E T E E E N R H A R
R O R R J N V W T D R A A R U
S O Y W P A P E R A M N L E P
F W E G R O E G L J W A L T Y
E N L A C I M E H C W I C K A
```

ALAMOGORDO (town)
ALBUQUERQUE (city)
ALPINE (tree)
ANTELOPE (animal)
AZTEC RUINS (monument)
BASIN range
Pinto BEAN (state vegetable)
Black BEAR (state animal)
CACTUS State
CARLSBAD Caverns National Park
CLOVIS (town)
Four CORNERS (4 states touch)
White-Tailed DEER (animal)

Living DESERT State Park
Land of ENCHANTMENT (nickname)
GOLD (mineral)
IT GROWS As It Goes (state motto)
LAS CRUCES (city)
MESILLA (town)
Museum of NEW MEXICO
NUT PINE (state tree)
O FAIR New Mexico (state song)
PIÑON (state tree)
Name: PLACE of the God (Aztec)

RIO RANCHO section
ROADRUNNER (state bird)
SANTA FE (capital)
Fort SELDEN
SILVER (mineral)
Blue SPRUCE (tree)
SUNSHINE State
TROUT (state fish)
TURQUOISE (state gem)
WHEELER Park (highest point)
YUCCA Flower (state flower)

```
A G R I O R A N C H O B E A R
Z L O A A N T E L O P E L W N
T T A L L E C U R P S B H P C
E N D M D P E A R R U E E L N
C E R X O F I N L Q E S O A E
R M U I A G I N U L U V I C D
U T N T C S O E E T I O L E L
I N N O A F R R C S P S I I E
N A E B A Q P A D Y C I E S S
S H R I U I C T U O R T N M E
W C R E N D O C I X E M W E N
E N M O E N C O R N E R S W A
X E N E L A S C R U C E S O E
C A R L S B A D E S E R T W B
S E N I H S N U S W O R G T I
```

NEW YORK

Entered Union: July 26, 1788 (#11)
Land Size: #30

ALBANY (capital)
APPLE (state)
Nat'l BASEBALL Hall of Fame
BEAR Mountain State Park
BEAVER (state animal)
Buffalo BILLS (football)
BINGHAMTON (city)
BLUEBIRD (state bird)
BRONX (NYC borough)
BUFFALO (city)
CHEESE (product)
DUKE of York (name)
ELLIS island (immigrant museum)
EMPIRE STATE
Lake ERIE

FINGER Lakes
FRANKLIN Roosevelt (born in Hyde Park)
GLENS Falls (town)
HOGS (livestock)
HOWE Cavern
HUDSON River
I LOVE New York (state song)
Statue of LIBERTY
Sugar MAPLE (state tree)
Mt. MARCY (highest point)
MARIST College
MILK (state beverage)
MILLARD Fillmore (born in Locke)
NEW YORK CITY (city)

NIAGARA Falls
Hyde PARK (FDR home)
PUMPKIN (crop)
ROME (town)
ROSE (state flower)
Ever UPWARD (state motto)
VASSAR College
WALL Street (financial center)
WEST POINT Military Academy
WOODSTOCK (concert site)
YONKERS (city)

```
E O R X Y Y T R E B I L L A W
N B L E N O T M A H G N I B R
U I E A K O N Y C R A M N A E
P L B P F U R K Y H R W S R H
W L E S A F D B E A E S I U O
A S W T D R U O E R A E D E W
R P L Y A R K B L V S S S R E
D G P L Y T I C K R O Y W E N
R H L L A R S B O N O L A V I
O I O E E B E E E T N S I A A
M J R G N L E L R U S K E E G
E K N O S S P S L I L D C B A
N I K P M U P A A I P B O K R
F R A N K L I N M B S M R O A
M A R I S T N I O P T S E W W
```

APPLE (crop)
BEAR Creek (town)
BLOWING Rock (natural formation)
BLUE RIDGE Mountains
CAPE Hatteras (National Seashore)
CARDINAL (state bird)
CHAPEL Hill (town)
CHARLOTTE (city)
DEER (animal)
DOGWOOD (state flower)
DUKE University
DURHAM (city)
FT. BRAGG

FURNITURE (product)
GREAT Smoky Mountains (National Park)
Kitty HAWK (1st plane flight)
HONEYBEE (state insect)
Andrew JOHNSON (born in Raleigh)
Mt. MITCHELL (highest point)
NANTAHALA Gorge
NEUSE River
NORTH CAROLINA
OLD NORTH State (state song)
PEANUT (crop)

PEE DEE River
PIEDMONT
PINE (state tree)
James POLK (born in Mecklenberg)
RALEIGH (capital)
ROANOKE Rapids (town)
TAR HEELS State
TO BE, RATHER THAN To Seem (state motto)
TRYON Palace (past Governors' mansion)
TURTLE (state reptile)
WINSTON-SALEM (city)

```
N P L C E E B Y E N O H H N E
O O E L H N P L E K U D A E R
Y L R P E E D E E L O H W U U
R K D T A H R T O P T N K S T
T O A N H C C C G R A R A E I
T R U A O C A T E N E H U O N
A T C L L R A H I J I E C T R
R P R H D A T R O M G W D R U
H H I I A A H H O D E U O D F
E G N E R R N A I L R L O L T
E A I E D S L R T H I G P A B
L T B E O M E O A N W N C P R
S O N N L U O M T O A R A L A
T I M E L A S N O T S N I W G
P A C B E A R D T A E R G O G
```

AMERICAN ELM (state tree)
ANTELOPE (animals)
BADLANDS
BEAVER (animal)
BISMARCK (capital)
BOTTINEAU (town)
CENTER of North America
DEER (animal)
DEVILS Lake (town)
FARGO (city)
FLICKERTAIL State Name: FRIENDS (Sioux Indian)
GRAND FORKS (city)
North Dakota HERITAGE Center

LAND of the Dakotas State
LIBERTY And Union, Now And Forever, One And Inseparable (state motto)
Western MEADOWLARK (state bird)
MILK (state beverage)
MISSOURI River
NORTH DAKOTA Hymn (state song)
OATS (crop)
PEACE GARDEN State
Northern PIKE (state fish)
Wild PRAIRIE Rose (state flower)
Wild RICE River

Writing ROCK (glacial boulder)
SIOUX State
SOURIS River
(ND) STATE University
New TOWN (town)
TURTLE Mountains
UNION Museum (Grand Forks)
WALSH County
WHEAT (crop)
WHITE BUTTE (highest point)
WILLISTON (town)

```
D C T H B O T T I N E A U D N
R E E D E T U R T L E R E O F
E N R X M T D O I G G V R L O
P T E R U L A B A R I T I G N
O E V C T O E T A L H C R I O
L R A H I R I N S D K A E R M
E N E C T R D S A E F I T U E
T K B Y E F A K R C R S T O A
N W C H O G O T L I I I U S D
A A M R S T A O A P E R B S O
N L K I A I A R N I N U E I W
O S K K L M P E D K D O T M L
I H R O C K S A H E S S I O A
N O T S I L L I W W N O H N R
U S D N A L D A B T T O W N K
```

OHIO

Entered Union: Mar. 1, 1803 (#17)
Land Size: #35

AKRON (city)
ANTIOCH College
BEAUTIFUL OHIO (state song)
BOWLING Green State University
BUCKEYE State
CARDINAL (state bird)
CEDAR Point (amusement park)
CINCINNATI (city)
CLEVELAND (city)
COLISEUM (basketball Cavaliers)
COLUMBUS (capital)
COTTONTAIL Rabbit (animal)
DAYTON (city)

White-Tailed DEER (animal)
Lake ERIE
Ohio FLINT (state gem)
James GARFIELD (born in Orange)
GATEWAY To The West
Ulysses S. GRANT (born in Point Pleasant)
Pro Football HALL of Fame
Warren G. HARDING (born in Corsica)
Rutherford HAYES (born in Delaware township)
Campbell HILL (highest point)
William MCKINLEY (born in Niles)
MILK (product)

NOTRE Dame College
Cincinnati REDS (baseball)
RIVERFRONT Stadium (Cincinnati)
SCARLET Carnation (state flower)
William TAFT (born in Cincinnati)
TOLEDO Museum of Art
TOMATO juice (state beverage)
WITH GOD ALL Things Are Possible (state motto)
YOUNGSTOWN (city)

```
Y C Y E L N I K C M I L K E B
A O L V F Y K S U D N A S E D
W T T A T E Y E K C U B A C N
E T F G N N S D E R T U N O L
T O A N T I O C H E T O R L I
A N T T L U D R L I T K A U T
G T I O C L T R F Y A H B M A
A A C L B H A U A R S S O B N
R I E E F C L D G C E O W U N
F L D D S O O N O M Y V L S I
I L A O H G I T O G A L I E C
E I R I R D J N A T H K N R N
L H O A R E E D P M R T G I I
D D N A L E V E L C O E I E C
A T H R I Y O U N G S T O W N
```

ARKANSAS River
Tulsa BALLET Theater
BARLEY (crop)
White BASS (state fish)
BISON (animal)
BLACK MESA (highest point)
BROKEN Arrow (city)
American *BUFFALO* (state animal)
Oklahoma CITY (capital)
Meat CLEAVER shape
COLE (town)
Nat'l COWBOY Hall Of Fame
ENID (city)
FAXON (town)

Scissor-Tailed FLYCATCHER (state bird)
FORT SMITH (national historic site)
GILCREASE Institute Of American History And Art
Softball HALL of Fame
Oklahoma HERITAGE Center
HOGS (livestock)
HONEYBEE (state insect)
HOWDY Folks (state poem)
LABOR CONQUERS All Things (state motto)
MISTLETOE (state flower)
MOOSE (animal)
MYRAID Convention Center

NORMAN (city)
OKLAHOMA (state song)
OZARK Mountains
PEEK (town)
PETROLEUM (product)
PHILBROOK Art Center
REDBUD (state tree)
Will ROGERS Memorial
SHEEP (livestock)
SOONER State
Rainbow TROUT (fish)
TULSA (city)

```
N B A L L E T S A S N A K R A
O U O K M U E L O R T E P O S
X F S L O B S H E E P M B E E
A F A R A H C D N E I R E S M
F A T S E C B I E S O E N A K
O L S O O U D K T K B A R E C
R O Y L D R Q L E Y M K O R A
T E E C U I E N E R A C G C L
S G V L A T A N O M L O E L B
M A K A O T O N O C A W R I A
I T Y E E H C H H O R B S G R
T I D O S L A H Z E S O O M L
H R W G L L C A E H N Y B A E
M E O A K M R M Y R A I D A Y
A H H O A K O O R B L I H P L
```

OREGON

Entered Union: Feb. 14, 1859 (#33)
Land Size: #10

ANTELOPE (animal)
Mt. ASHLAND
ASTORIA (city)
BARLEY (crop)
BEAVER State
Swallowtail BUTTERFLY (insect)
CASCADE Range
CHEESE (product)
CHICKEN (livestock)
CHINOOK Salmon (state fish)
CHRISTMAS trees (product)
COLUMBIA River
CRATER Lake

CULP Creek (town)
DAIRY (products)
DOUGLAS FIR (state tree)
Oregon GRAPE (state flower)
Sea LION Caves
LUMBER (product)
MILK (product)
OREGON, MY Oregon (state song)
PORTLAND (City)
REED College
ROGUE River Valley
SALEM (capital)
SHRIMP (product)

STEENS Mountain
SUGAR beets (crop)
SUNSET State
TROY (town)
TUNA (fish)
UNION (state motto)
VALENTINE State
WESTERN Meadowlark (state bird)
WHEAT (crop)
WILLIAMETTE River Valley
WOOL (product)
YODER (town)

```
R  C  A  S  C  A  D  E  A  N  U  T  D  E  O
C  P  H  D  N  A  L  T  R  O  P  O  B  R  E
E  R  M  E  M  R  E  E  D  E  U  E  A  O  P
L  L  A  I  E  E  T  G  P  G  V  G  R  G  O
N  O  O  T  R  S  L  O  L  A  U  A  L  R  L
N  C  O  Y  E  H  E  A  L  S  R  C  E  G  E
D  E  H  W  L  R  S  E  S  C  S  G  Y  B  T
T  A  K  R  E  F  N  R  U  N  O  N  R  A  N
R  E  I  C  I  T  R  L  E  N  M  A  C  I  A
T  E  S  R  I  S  P  E  M  B  I  N  H  B  S
R  A  B  N  Y  H  T  Y  T  R  L  O  I  M  H
O  Y  E  M  U  S  C  M  O  T  K  I  N  U  L
G  O  G  H  U  S  O  T  A  D  U  L  O  L  A
U  R  O  E  W  L  S  A  E  S  E  B  O  O  N
E  T  T  E  M  A  I  L  L  I  W  R  K  C  D
```

41

ALLEGHENY River
APPLE (crop)
Liberty BELL
BLUE Mountains
James BUCHANAN (born by Mercersburg)
CHOCOLATE (product)
COAL (product)
Great DANE (state dog)
DRAKE Well Museum
DREXEL University
Philadelphia EAGLES (football)
EGGS (product)
ERIE (city)

Ruffed GROUSE (state bird)
GROVE City (town)
Independence HALL
HARRISBURG (capital)
HAZLETON (town)
HEMLOCK (state tree)
KEYSTONE State
Mountain LAUREL (state flower)
NEW CASTLE (town)
OHIO River
PENNSYLVANIA (state song)
PHILADELPHIA (city)
Philadelphia PHILLIES (baseball)

PITTSBURGH (city)
POCONOS (mountains)
READING (city)
Three RIVERS Stadium (baseball)
SCRANTON (city)
Brook TROUT (state fish)
VALLEY Forge (town)
VIRTUE, LIBERTY, And Independence (state motto)
Name: WOODS (sylvania - Latin)

```
K N R I V E R S E I L L I H P
C A I H P L E D A L I H P E O
O P Y N E H G E L L A I N E C
L P T E E D Y K L N T N S V O
M L R L L U S N E T S U A W N
E E E A G L L E S Y O G O V O
H N B U D R A B L R S O G R S
A E I R E R U V G G D T E E T
Z W L E N R A B L S A A O E D
L C E L G N E K S A D E V N R
E A U H I L P A E I O O P A E
T S T A L N O T N A R C S D X
O T R L E I N G Y G N R S E E
N L I L H A B U C H A N A N L
S E V O V L E T A L O C O H C
```

42

RHODE ISLAND

Entered Union: May 29, 1790 (#13)
Land Size: #50

ARCADE (1st US indoor mall, 1828)
BROWN University
BRYANT College
Rhode Island Red CHICKEN (state bird)
EAST Beach
Int'l Tennis Hall of FAME
FISHERMEN'S Memorial State Park
HOPE (state motto)
Newport JAZZ Festival
JERIMOTH Hill (highest point)

LITTLE RHODY (nickname)
MILK (product)
MUSEUM of (RI) History
NARRAGANSETT Bay
NEWPORT (city)
NINIGRET Park Nat'l Wildlife Refuge
OCEAN State
PAWTUCKET (city)
PIGS (livestock)
PLANTATION State
POINT Judith (town)
PROVIDENCE (capital)
PRUDENCE Island

QUEEN River
RED MAPLE (state tree)
RHODE ISLAND (state song)
Seekonk RIVER
SCITUATE Reservoir
SHEEP (livestock)
SMITH and Sayles Reservoir
VIOLET (state flower)
WARWICK (city)
WOONSOCKET (city)
YACHT Races

```
P D S C I T U A T E D A C R A
O R I V E R T J L E N L H H T
E T O R S H E P C O I O T R S
M E N V C R A N I T D E O M W
A K A A I M E T T E R P I U O
F C Y M D D A L I G W T W E O
I U O E U T E S I E H R A S N
S T R R N R L N N Q S H R U S
H W P A H A I H C U T G W M O
E A L O N N B B N E K C I H C
R P D D L D O R L E P L C P K
M Y L N A E C O Y N K O K O E
E S H E E P I W J A Z Z H I T
N T S A E V E N H M N O E N O
S N A R R A G A N S E T T T E
```

43

SOUTH CAROLINA

Entered Union: May 23, 1788 (#8)
Land Size: #40

BIRD Island
BLACK River
BLUE Ridge Mountains
CAROLINA (state song)
CHARLESTON Museum (oldest in US, 1773)
CLARK Hill Reservoir
CLEMSON University
COLUMBIA (capital)
CORN (crop)
COTTON (crop)
CRABS (fish)
DAIRY (products)
EGGS (products)
HOGS (livestock)
Andrew JACKSON (born in Waxhaw)

Bob JONES University
LAKE Marion
South Carolina on My MIND (state song)
MYRTLE Beach
PALMETTO (state tree)
College PARK Stadium
PEACH (state fruit)
PEE DEE River
PORT Royal Sound
PREPARED in Mind and Resources (state motto)
RICE State
RILEY Park
ROCK HILL (town)
SASSAFRAS Mountain (highest point)

SAXON (town)
SOUTH Carolina
Boykin SPANIEL (state dog)
Southern 500 STOCK Car Race
STRIPED BASS (state fish)
WHEAT (crop)
WHILE (I) Breathe, (I) Hope (state motto)
WHITE-TAILED Deer (state animal)
WILD Turkey (game bird)
Carolina WREN (state bird)
YELLOW Jessamine (state flower)

```
C R T A E H W I L D A I R Y S
L A I B M U L O C I D E U L B
N O X A S L K U L E O S P C A
P I H E S R L R L L A R O H R
H A N T A U S I A N E R W B C
N O L E B C A P H P N Y L T H
J S G M D T A T A K R A L C A
D G O S E C I R S N C U P O R
S N B T P T E K O K I O A J L
W C I I I D T C U L R E R A E
T H R M R R E O T T I P L C S
W O I A T D K T H N E N N K T
H U L L S S A S S A F R A S O
P E E D E E L I C L E M S O N
L M Y R T L E H C O T T O N R
```

ABERDEEN (city)
AUGUSTANA College
BLACK HILLS Spruce (state tree)
BURKE (town)
CORN (crop)
COTTONWOOD (town)
COYOTE State
CRAZY Horse (memorial)
DELL Rapids (town)
GOLD (mineral)
GRAND River
GREAT Plains
HAIL, South Dakota (state song)

HARNEY Peak (highest point)
HURON (town)
LAKE Oahe
LUMBER
MEAT (industry)
MILK (product)
MOUNT RUSHMORE (memorial)
NATIONAL College
NORTHERN State College
PARKER Peak
PASQUE FLOWER (state flower)
Ring-Necked PHEASANT (state bird)

PIERRE (capital)
PINE RIDGE (town)
RAPID City (city)
Rose QUARTZ (state mineral)
SILVER (mineral)
SIOUX FALLS (city)
SOUTH DAKOTA
Big STONE Lake
UNDER GOD The People Rule (state motto)
WHEAT (crop)
WIND CAVE

```
K S L L A F X U O I S O C G N
T M O U N T R U S H M O R E R
D N L U M B E R T S Y E W G E
O K A S T O N E U O A I T D H
O L K S M H U N T T N A B I T
W L E B A O D E H D E U L R R
N E E D R E B A C M R G A E O
O D N A R G H A K K G U C N N
T A Z G R A V P E O S S K I A
T U O T R E M I L K T T H P T
O D N N R K V D C A D A I A I
C T E R H A K L E R I N L R O
S Y E N O R U H I L A A L K N
D I P A R C W Q D S U Z S E A
P A S Q U E F L O W E R Y R L
```

AGRICULTURE And Commerce (state motto)
Tenn. - AMERICA at its Best (state motto)
ANDREW Johnson National Monument
BIG BEND State
BRYAN College
COAL (mineral)
COPPER (mineral)
COUNTRY Music
EAST Tennessee State University
1982 World's FAIR
GRACELAND (Elvis Presley mansion)
GREAT Smoky Mountains National Park

IRIS (state flower)
KING College
KNOXVILLE (city)
LADYBUG (state insect)
LIBERTY Bowl
LOOKOUT Mountain
MEMPHIS (city)
MIDDLE Tenn. State University
MOCKINGBIRD (state bird)
MONTGOMERY Bell Park
NASHVILLE (capital)
PARIS (town)
PEARL (state gem)
PINE Mountain
Tulip POPLAR (state tree)

RACCOON (state wild animal)
Tenn. Valley RAILROAD Museum
SHILOH (town)
SHORT Mountain
8 STATES (border)
My TENNESSEE (state song)
Tennessee VALLEY Authority
VANDERBILT University
Tennessee WALTZ (state song)
WHEN IT'S Iris Time In Tennessee (state song)
ZINC (mineral)

```
N T M B I G B E N D T S M B A
Y W E R D N A E N S E O R G G
T H M N Z T L A W T C Y R R N
R E P E N A L S A K A I E E I
E N H T O E H T I N C A L P K
B I I C C O S N A U T L O P M
I T S A L P G S L P I A O O O
L S R I A B H T E V M D K C N
A G H R I V U A X E A N O N T
D S I R I R R O R O M U U I G
Y S D L E L N I R I N E T Z O
B F L E N K C L D T R O H S M
U E A N I A I D R A L P O P E
G S T I P A L Y N O O C C A R
T L I B R E D N A V A L L E Y
```

ALAMO Museum
ALLEY Theatre
AMARILLO (city)
AMON Carter Museum
ARLINGTON Stadium (baseball)
AUSTIN (capital)
Toledo BEND Reservoir
BLUEBONNET (state flower)
CASS County
CHICKEN (livestock)
COTTON Bowl
Dallas COWBOYS (football)
DALLAS (leading city)
Dwight EISENHOWER (born in Denison)

EL PASO (city)
FAIR Park (State Fair, Dallas)
FRIENDSHIP (state motto)
HOUSTON (city)
LAKE Texarkana
LAMAR University
LAREDO (city)
LONE STAR State
LYNDON JOHNSON (born in Johnson City)
MIDLAND (city)
MOCKINGBIRD (state bird)
NASA Headquarters (Houston)
Texas, OUR TEXAS (state song)

PECAN (state tree)
Texas RANGERS (baseball)
REUNION Arena
RICE University
Dallas STARS (hockey)
SULPHUR River
Texas TECH University
TOPAZ (state gem)
Lake TRAVIS
TRINITY River
WACO (city)
WITTE Museum (San Antonio)

```
C N O S N H O J N O D N Y L T
S O A B L U E B O N N E T I S
R L T C N O T S U O H T U N Y
O E A T E N E K C I H C O T O
L S W R O P C M S N O M I H B
L A A O E N I T S U A N C N W
I T K P H D R H R E I E O A O
R R R E L N O T S R T T L R C
A O A A O E E A T D G O A O A
M E N M V X N S S N N N P C S
A D A X A I A A I E G E A A S
F L B S Y L S L S E T T I W Z
A Y E L L A R T R A S T A R S
I X N A O A A S U L P H U R F
R E D T D R I B G N I K C O M
```

UTAH

Entered Union: Jan. 4, 1896 (#45)
Land Size: #12

BEAR River
BEAVER River
BEEHIVE State
Cedar BREAKS National Monument
BRIGHAM Young University
BRYCE Canyon National Park
COPPER (mineral)
Utah Repertory DANCE Theatre
Museum of FINE Arts
GOLDEN SPIKE National Historic Site
GREAT Salt Lake
HOGS (livestock)
HONEYBEE (state insect)
INDUSTRY (state motto)

KINGS Peak (highest point)
LEHI (town)
METAL (products)
MORMON Tabernacle Choir
NEPHI (town)
OGDEN (city)
Salt PALACE (arena)
PHEASANT (game bird)
PINE Valley Mountains
PROVO (city)
RAINBOW Bridge (stone bridge)
SALT LAKE CITY (capital)
SEA GULL (state bird)
SEGO LILY (state flower)
SHEEP (livestock)

Bonneville Salt Flats SPEEDWAY
Blue SPRUCE (state tree)
Utah STATE University
Utah SYMPHONY
TIMPANOGOS Cave National Monument
TOPAZ (state gem)
Rainbow TROUT (state fish)
UTAH Lake
Utah, WE LOVE THEE (state song)
WEBER State College
WEST Valley City (city)
ZION National Park

```
K B E A V E R T N A S A E H P
O R P A L A C E M A H G I R B
Y A W D E E P S P Z A P O T R
P L K C W E S T W P G V A I Y
E V I H E E B Y E N O H U M C
M S N L L U C H B E L C S P E
O T G L O E T U E N D R Y A I
R A S G V G C A R I E A M N N
M T D T E L E N H P N I P O D
O E U N T B L S A W S N H G U
N G I B H M R U A D P B O O S
E F R A E B E E G Z I O N S T
P H P E E H S T A A K W Y U R
H C T S A L T L A K E C I T Y
I T U O R T I H E L S S G O H
```

VERMONT

Entered Union: Mar. 4, 1791 (#14)
Land Size: #43

St. ALBANS (town)
BARRE (town)
BEAVERS (animals)
BENNINGTON (city)
BURLINGTON (city)
CALVIN COOLIDGE (born in Plymouth Notch)
CHESTER ARTHUR (born in Fairfield)
Red CLOVER (state flower)
COLCHESTER (town)
DAIRY (products)

ESSEX (town)
FAIRBANKS MUSEUM of Nat'l Science
FREEDOM And Unity (state motto)
GREEN Mountain State
HAIL, VERMONT! (state song)
HERMIT Thrush (state bird)
HONEYBEE (state insect)
Morgan HORSE (state animal)
LAMOILLE River

Mt. MANSFIELD (highest point)
MAPLE Syrup (product)
MONTPELIER (capital)
NORWICH University
OTTER Creek
RUTLAND (city)
SKIING
SUGAR MAPLE (state tree)
WHITE River
WINDSOR (town)

```
M E R U H T R A R E T S E H C
U R L M H E S R O H E E E O A
E V O L A K T N B L B R L M L
S N W H I T E E P Y M C R V V
U O R I L O A A E I H E M M I
M T N N V V M N T E V S O A N
S G R O E E O A S O U N D N C
K N O R R H R T L G T E E S O
N I S W M U E C A P N E E F O
A N D I O R T R E L M R R I L
B N N C N N M L E R B G F E I
R E I H T A I S A T R A E L D
I B W V P E S M R N T A N D G
A M E L R E Y R I A D O B S E
F V E V X B U R L I N G T O N
```

AMERICAN Dogwood (state flower)
Richmond BALLET
Natural BRIDGE (from rock)
CALFEE Park
CARDINAL (state bird)
CARRY ME BACK To Old Virginia (state song)
Richmond COLISEUM
COMMONWEALTH
DOGWOOD (state tree)
American FOXHOUND (state dog)
FREDERICKSBURG (town)
FRONT Royal (town)

GEORGE Washington (born in Westmoreland County)
GLEN Allen (town)
GOODE (town)
IRON Mountains
KERR Reservoir
LONG Branch (town)
James MADISON (born in Port Conway)
James MONROE (born in Westmoreland County)
MONTICELLO (Jefferson home)
MOTHER of States (nickname)
MOUNT VERNON (town)

Newport NEWS (city)
OLD DOMINION State
St. PAUL'S College
POTOMAC River
RICHMOND (capital)
ROANOKE (city)
Mt. ROGERS (highest point)
SALEM Municipal Field
SHEEP (livestock)
THUS EVER To Tyrants (state motto)
John TYLER (born in Greenway)
VIRGINIA BEACH (city)

```
D R E V E S U H T N O R F F G
O N E W S R E K O N A O R R T
G O O D E E F L A C X E R E M
W N N C G L E N H D E L O O
O R A E N O R I O E K L T V N
O E C O R R L U R C A H G I T
D V I R G I N I A B E A C H I
A T R N A D C B S R N A A B C
E N E O I K E H E E M R R M E
G U M M S M P L M O U I D A L
R O A B Y A Y G T O D M I D L
O M U R U T L O N G N V N I O
E R R L I N P E E H S D A S N
G A S N O I N I M O D D L O G
C O M M O N W E A L T H I N R
```

Entered Union: Nov. 11, 1889 (#42)
Land Size: #20

APPLE (fruit)
BASTYR College
BELLEVUE (city)
BELLINGHAM (town)
BLUE Mountains
BY AND BY (state motto)
CHENEY Stadium
DAIRY (product)
EVERETT Memorial Stadium
EVERGREEN State
HOGS (livestock)
KINGDOME (baseball)
MILK (product)
MOSES Lake

Museum Of NATIVE
  American Cultures
NORTH Cascades National
  Park
OLYMPIA (capital)
Seattle OPERA
PACIFIC Ocean
PARKER Field
PEARS (crop)
Only PRESIDENT name state
University Of PUGET Sound
Pink RHODODENDRON
  (state flower)
RUBY Beach

SALMON (product)
SEATTLE (city)
SPOKANE (city)
Washington STATE
  University
STEELHEAD trout (state fish)
TACOMA (city)
WALLA WALLA (town)
WASHINGTON, My Home
  (state song)
WESTERN HEMLOCK (state
  tree)
WILLOW Goldfinch (state
  bird)

```
W A N O R D N E D O D O H R O
D A T T N E E R G R E V E U K
A S S E Y R Y T S A B K A B C
E L A H G B L U E G R M P Y O
H M L L I U D S G A O A P P L
L N I A M N P N P C E H L R M
E T O L W O G G A U S G E E E
E S Y R K A N T V Y C N V S H
T S E A T T L E O I B I E I N
S R N S S H L L F N T L R D R
T E E P O L Y I A A S L E E E
A I H H E M C W N W W E T N T
T N C B P A D A I R Y B T T S
E A I I P H R K I N G D O M E
N R A R E P O S N W O L L I W
```

WEST VIRGINIA

Entered Union: June 20, 1863 (#35)
Land Size: #41

Mountaineers Are ALWAYS Free Men (state motto)
APPLE (state fruit)
BLACK BEAR (state animal)
BLUE Hole (spring)
BOWEN Field
CARDINAL (state bird)
CATTLE (livestock)
CHARLESTON (capital)
CHEMICALS (products)
COAL (product)
Huntington CUBS (minor league baseball)
GLASS marbles (product)

HARPERS Ferry Historical Park
HIGHEST state e. of Mississippi
West Virginia, My HOME Sweet Home (state song)
HUNNICUTT Field
Spruce KNOB (highest point)
LAKE Erie
Big LAUREL (state flower)
MARSHALL University
MONONGAHELA National Forest
MOUNTAIN State
OHIO River

PRINCETON Reds (minor league baseball)
RHODODENDRON (Big Laurel)
Kanawha RIVER
Big SANDY River
SUGAR MAPLE (state tree)
THIS IS MY West Virginia (state song)
Brook TROUT (state fish)
WATT Powell Park
WEST VIRGINIA Hills (state song)
WHEELING (city)

```
R E V I R T E B W T E U L B T
R L N W A T T H O L A O C H B
G P O A V S E U P N S E I O C
N A T I I E Y P C R K S W H A
O M E S L N A A A I I E A W R
R R C I S N I E W S N R L T D
D A N H L A B G M L L N A S I
N G I N A K L Y R E A N U E N
E U R G C R H G S I R I R H A
D S P A I O P T T S V A E G L
O I L N M I O E I R A T L I A
D B A E E N V T R S O N S H K
O L L A H S R A M S H U D E E
H S B U C A T T L E I O T Y W
R A L E H A G N O N O M S A W
```

BADGER State
BASS (fish product)
BELOIT College
BLUE River (town)
BRADLEY Center
BRULE River
Milwaukee BUCKS (basketball)
CHEESE (product)
CORN (crop)
COWS (livestock)
DAIRY (products)
White-tailed DEER (state wild animal)
EGGS (product)
FORWARD (state motto)
GOODLAND Field

Name: GRASSY Place (Chippewa)
GREAT Lakes
GREEN BAY (port)
HONEYBEE (state insect)
HUDSON (town)
Dard HUNTER Paper Museum
ICE AGE National Scenic Trail
LITTLE Chute (town)
MACHINERY (products)
MADISON (capital)
MARQUETTE University
MILWAUKEE (city)
MUENSTER Cheese (product)
NICOLET National Forest

ON, WISCONSIN! (state song)
Green Bay PACKERS (football)
RICE Lake
ROBIN (state bird)
SUGAR MAPLE (state tree)
TIMMS HILL (highest point)
TROUT (product)
TWIN Lakes (town)
Wood VIOLET (state flower)
WARNER Park
YUBA (town)

```
R  E  E  D  B  S  I  D  N  A  L  D  O  O  G
W  E  E  S  C  U  M  A  C  H  I  N  E  R  Y
E  A  G  K  E  E  C  U  N  I  W  T  H  W  U
E  T  R  G  U  E  G  K  E  I  N  U  I  E  B
B  E  E  N  S  A  H  A  S  N  N  O  N  C  A
Y  L  E  S  E  F  W  C  E  T  S  R  W  I  S
E  O  N  W  O  R  O  L  E  C  O  T  G  R  Y
N  I  B  O  R  N  I  R  I  C  I  R  E  S  E
O  V  A  T  S  T  T  T  W  M  E  K  S  R  L
H  E  Y  I  T  I  E  C  M  A  C  A  S  B  D
U  L  N  L  O  L  D  S  T  A  R  W  A  L  A
D  U  E  L  O  A  H  A  P  G  O  D  B  U  R
S  R  E  C  I  I  S  I  M  C  G  I  W  E  B
O  B  I  R  L  N  E  T  T  E  U  Q  R  A  M
N  N  Y  L  S  U  G  A  R  M  A  P  L  E  S
```

WYOMING

Entered Union: July 10, 1890 (#44)
Land Size: #9

BEANS (crop)
BEAR RIVER ranges
BELLE Fourche River
BOYSEN State Park
BUFFALO BILL Reservoir
CASPER (city)
CHEYENNE (capital)
CODY (town)
COTTONWOOD (state tree)
DEVILS Tower National Monument
Continental DIVIDE
EQUALITY State
FLAMING Gorge National Recreation Area

FORT Caspar Museum
GANNETT PEAK (highest point)
GRAND TETON National Park
GREEN River
INDIAN Paintbrush (state flower)
JACKSON HOLE Museum
KEYHOLE State Park
MOUNTAIN State
NORTH Platte River
OATS (crop)
POWDER River
Equal RIGHTS (state motto)

SALT River
SHERIDAN (city)
SHOSHONE National Forest
SNAKE River
THUNDER Basin Nat'l Grassland
WESTERN Meadowlark (state bird)
WHEAT (crop)
WIND River
WYOMING (state song)

```
S S T H G I R E V I R R A E B
G N N B E L L E S N A K E O U
C R T A A L R E P S A C Y W F
O E A S D O O P Y E O S F T F
T T E N N I O H P D E T L J A
T S H M D W R T Y N C A A I L
O E W I D T T E G E S C M S O
N W N E M E E L H L K O I S B
W E R O N O G T I S S D N H I
O G E N R N U V O N N I G O L
O A A R I T E N S N A V E S L
D G T M G D H Y T H E I N H I
N N O S F O R T E A B D D O B
I Y T I L A U Q E H I E W N M
W J R E D N U H T T C N O E I
```

Answers

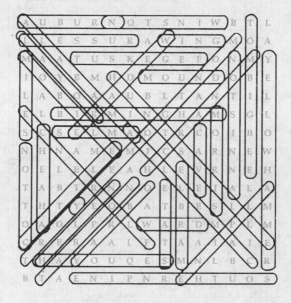

Alabama *(page 4)*

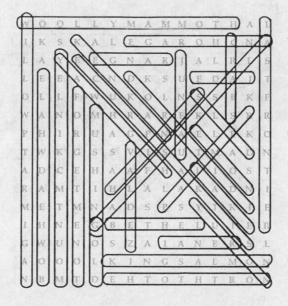

Alaska *(page 5)*

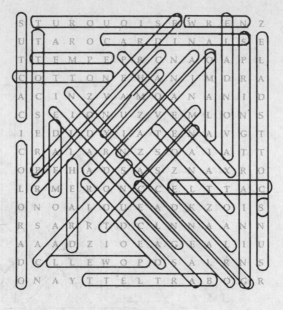

Arizona *(page 6)*

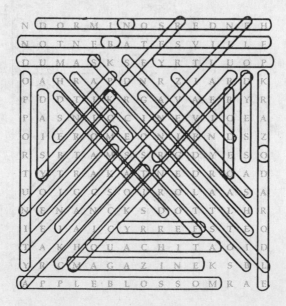

Arkansas *(page 7)*

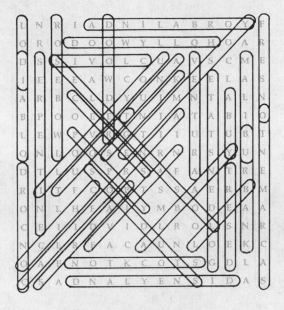

California *(page 8)*

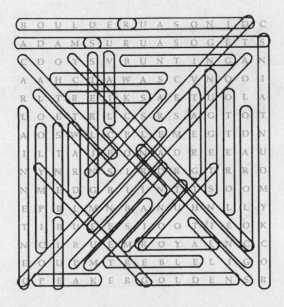

Colorado *(page 9)*

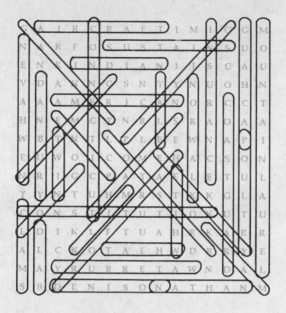

Connecticut *(page 10)*

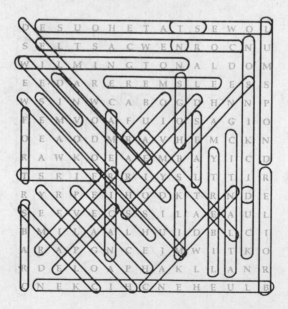

Delaware *(page 11)*

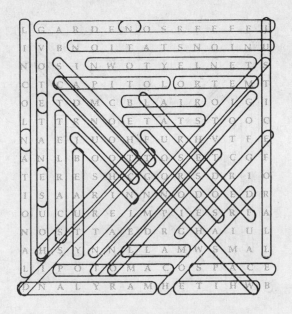

District of Columbia *(page 12)*

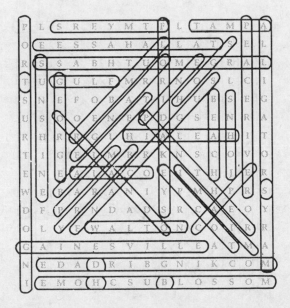

Florida *(page 13)*

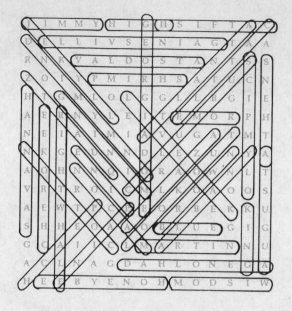

Georgia *(page 14)*

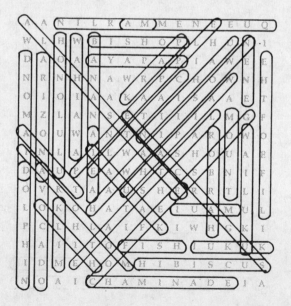

Hawaii *(page 15)*

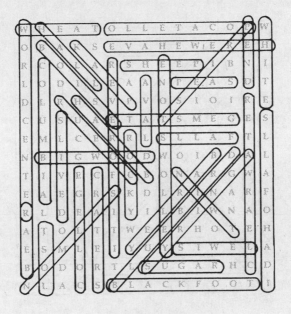

Idaho *(page 16)*

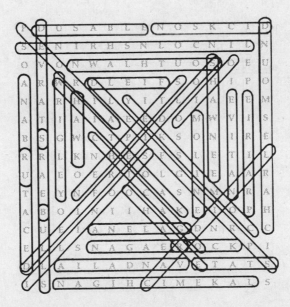

Illinois *(page 17)*

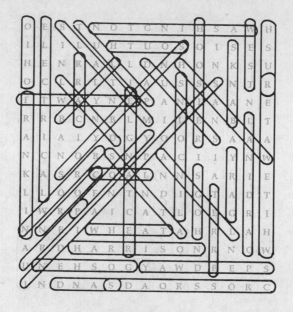

Indiana *(page 18)*

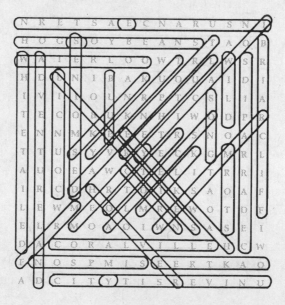

Iowa *(page 19)*

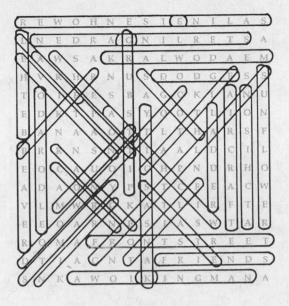

Kansas *(page 20)*

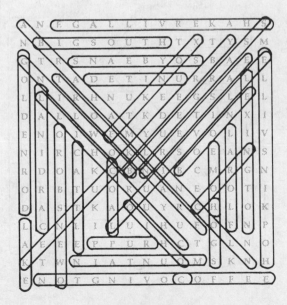

Kentucky *(page 21)*

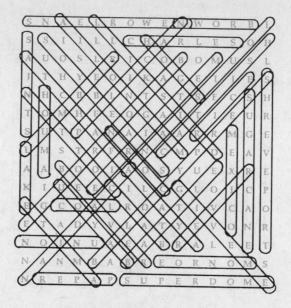

Louisiana *(page 22)*

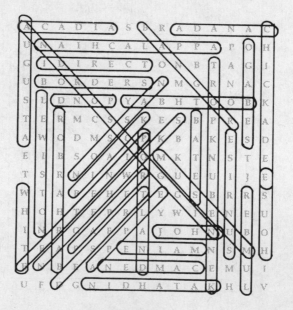

Maine *(page 23)*

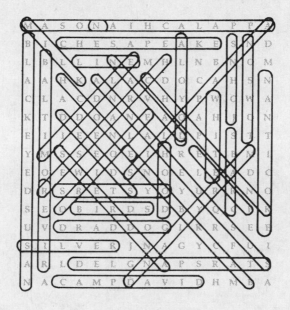

Maryland *(page 24)*

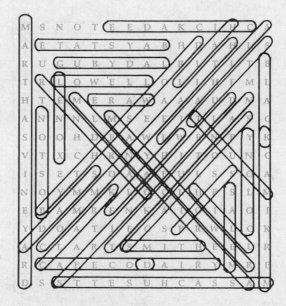

Massachusetts *(page 25)*

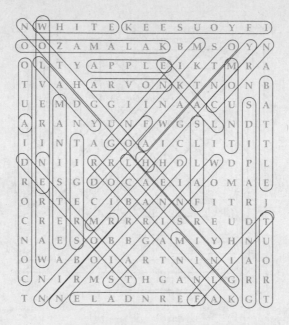

Michigan *(page 26)*

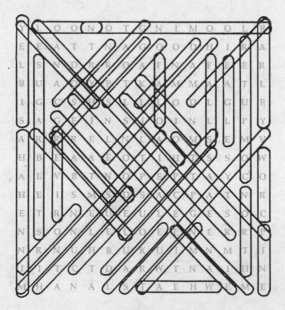

Minnesota *(page 27)*

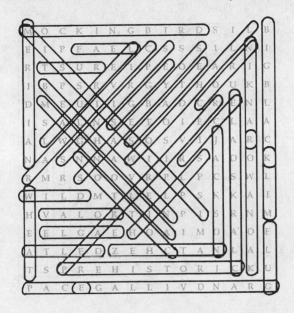

Mississippi *(page 28)*

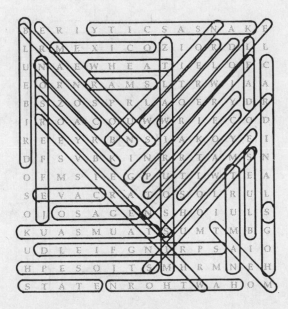

Missouri *(page 29)*

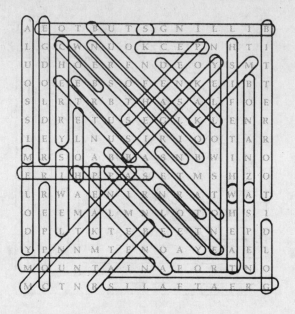

Montana *(page 30)*

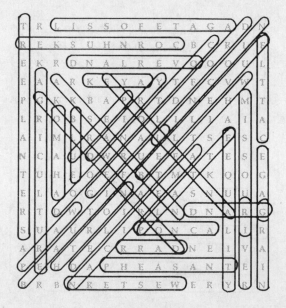

Nebraska *(page 31)*

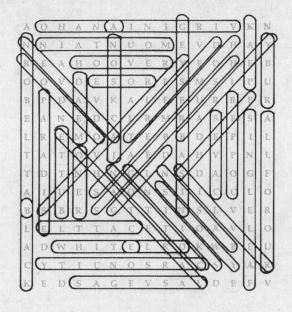

Nevada *(page 32)*

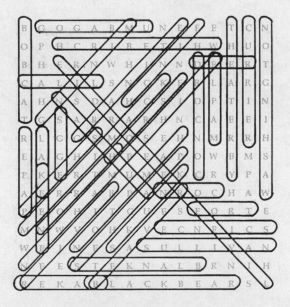

New Hampshire *(page 33)*

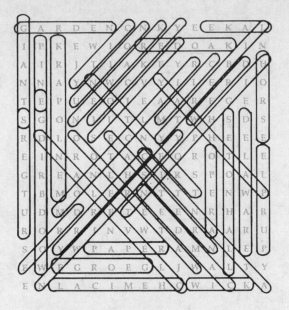

New Jersey *(page 34)*

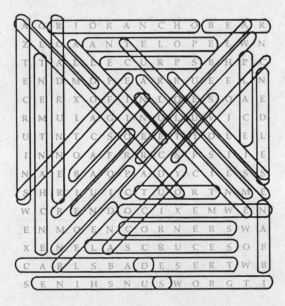

New Mexico *(page 35)*

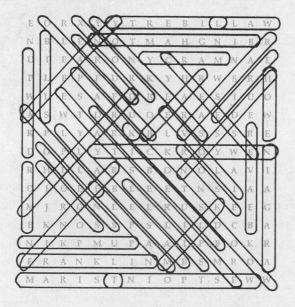

New York *(page 36)*

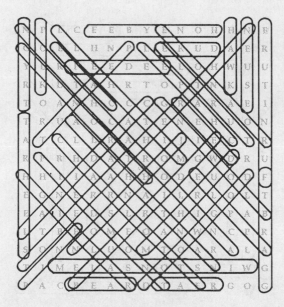

North Carolina *(page 37)*

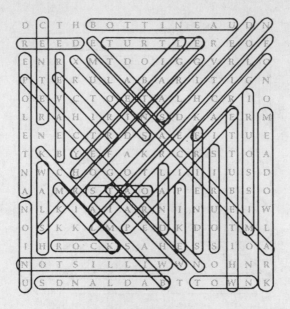

North Dakota *(page 38)*

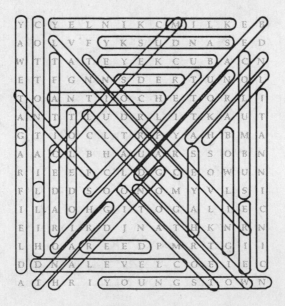

Ohio *(page 39)*

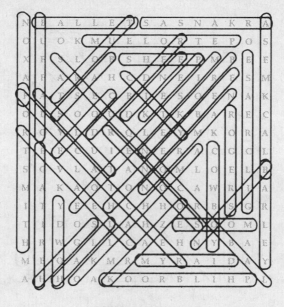

Oklahoma *(page 40)*

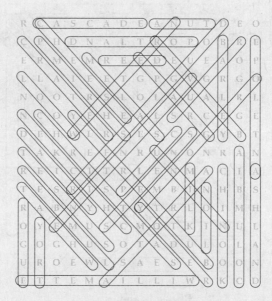

Oregon *(page 41)*

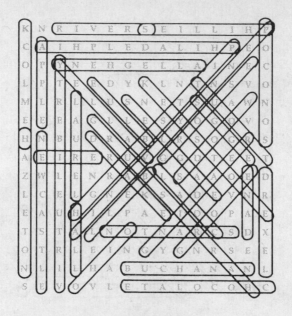

Pennsylvania *(page 42)*

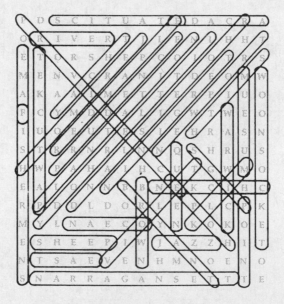

Rhode Island *(page 43)*

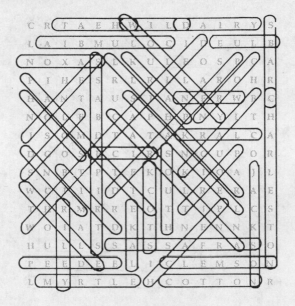

South Carolina *(page 44)*

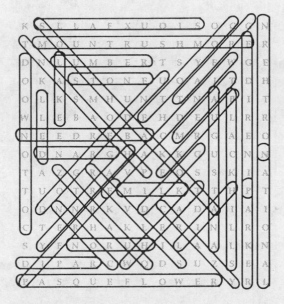

South Dakota *(page 45)*

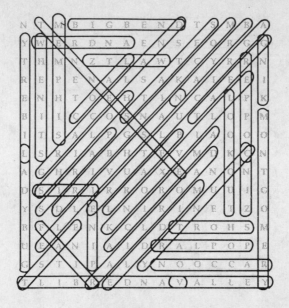

Tennessee *(page 46)*

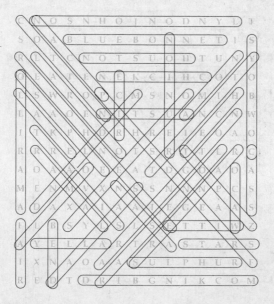

Texas *(page 47)*

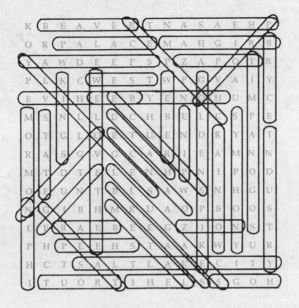

Utah *(page 48)*

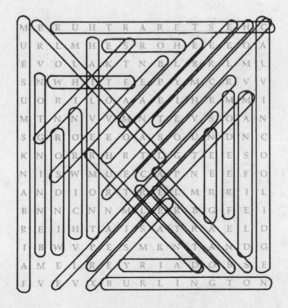

Vermont *(page 49)*

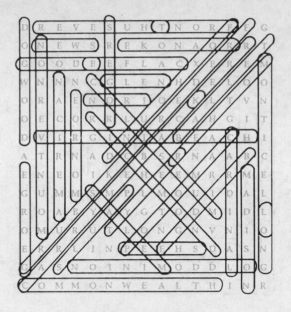

Virginia *(page 50)*

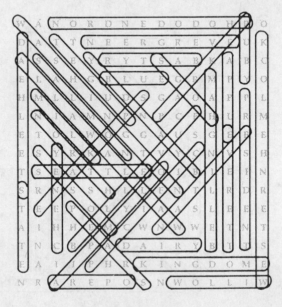

Washington *(page 51)*

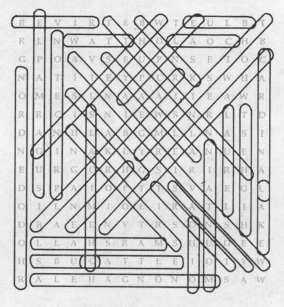

West Virginia *(page 52)*

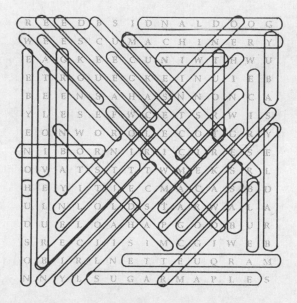

Wisconsin *(page 53)*

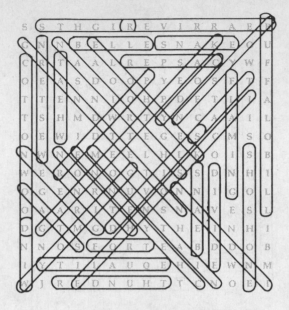

Wyoming *(page 54)*